Richard W White, William J Clements

Can a Negro Hold Office in Georgia?

Decided in Supreme Court of Georgia, June term, 1869. Arguments of council, with

the opinions of the judges, and the decision of court in the case of Richard W.

White, clerk of Superior Court of Chatham Co.

Richard W White, William J Clements

Can a Negro Hold Office in Georgia?
Decided in Supreme Court of Georgia, June term, 1869. Arguments of council, with the opinions of the judges, and the decision of court in the case of Richard W. White, clerk of Superior Court of Chatham Co.

ISBN/EAN: 9783337301279

Printed in Europe, USA, Canada, Australia, Japan

Cover: Foto ©ninafisch / pixelio.de

More available books at **www.hansebooks.com**

CAN A NEGRO HOLD OFFICE IN GEORGIA?

DECIDED IN SUPREME COURT OF GEORGIA, JUNE TERM, 1869.

ARGUMENTS OF COUNSEL,

WITH THE OPINIONS OF THE JUDGES, AND

THE DECISION OF COURT

IN THE CASE OF

RICHARD W. WHITE,
CLERK OF SUPERIOR COURT OF CHATHAM CO.,
Plaintiff in Error.

VERSUS

THE STATE OF GEORGIA, *Ex Relatione*
WM. J. CLEMENTS,
Defendant in Error.

QUO WARRANTO.

CHATHAM.

PHONOGRAPHICALLY REPORTED
BY EUGENE DAVIS.

ATLANTA, GA.:
DAILY INTELLIGENCER BOOK AND JOB OFFICE.
1869.

SUPREME COURT OF GEORGIA,

JUNE TERM, 1869.

Hon. JOSEPH E. BROWN, Chief Justice.
Hon. H. K. McCAY, } Associate Justices.
Hon. HIRAM WARNER, }

RICHARD W. WHITE,
Clerk of Superior Court of Chatham County,
Plaintiff in Error.

vs.

The State of Georgia. *Ex Relatione*
WM. J. CLEMENTS,
Defendant in Error.

Quo Warranto.

Chatham.

SUPREME COURT CHAMBERS,
ATLANTA, GA., June 9, 1869.

Col. A. W. STONE, in opening the case on behalf of the plaintiff in error, read the record of the Court below, which is as follows:

GEORGIA, }
CHATHAM COUNTY. }

To the Honorable the Judge of the Superior Court of said County :

The Petition of William J. Clements, a free white citizen of the said County of Chatham, respectfully shows, that he is above the age of twenty-one years, and in every other respect eligible to, and qualified to hold the office of Clerk of the Superior Court of the said County of Chatham, according to the laws of Georgia ; that at an election held in said County of Chatham on the 21st, 22d, 23d and 24th days of April, eighteen hundred and sixty-eight, for a Clerk of the Superior Court of said County of Chatham, pursuant to law, one Richard W. White, a person of color, and your petitioner, were the only persons voted for by the Electors ; that the said Richard W. White, a person of color, received the highest number of votes, and was commissioned as such Clerk, and is in the discharge of the duties and exercising the rights and powers, and receiving the emoluments incident and attached to said office. And your Petitioner further shows, that the said Richard W. White is a person of color, and has in his veins one-eighth of negro, or African, blood, and was consequently ineligible to the office of Clerk of said Court, and was, and still is, incompetent and unable, under the laws of Georgia, to hold said office.

And your Petitioner further shows, that by Section 121 of the Code of Georgia, it is enacted "that if at any popular election to fill any office the person elected is ineligible, the person having the next highest number of votes, who is eligible, whenever a plurality elects, shall be declared elected, and be duly qualified and commissioned to such office ; that your Petitioner was at the time of said election eligible to said office, and that a plurality elects in such election.

Wherefore your Petitioner prays the leave of your Honor to file an information in the name of the State, in the nature of a *quo warranto*, calling upon the said Richard W. White to show by virtue of what right or law he holds the above mentioned office, and why he should not be amoved therefrom and your Petitioner duly declared elected, and be qualified and commissioned as Clerk of the Superior Court of the County of Chatham for the term for which said Richard W. White has been commissioned.

And your Petitioner will ever pray, &c.

WM. J. CLEMENTS.

T. E. LLOYD, *Attorney.*

Personally came before me, William J. Clements, who, being duly sworn, deposes and says that the facts set forth in the above Petition are true.

Sworn to before me this January 22d, 1869.

HENRY S. WETMORE, WM. J. CLEMENTS.
Ordinary Chatham Co., Ga.

GEORGIA,   }
CHATHAM COUNTY. }

On reading the above Petition and Affidavit it is ordered that the said Richard W. White, now acting as Clerk of the Superior Court of Chatham County, do show cause before me, at the Court House, at Savannah, in said County, at eleven o'clock, A. M., on the 26th day of January, 1869, why an information in the nature of a *quo warranto* should not be filed against him as prayed for in said Petition, and that a copy of the Petition Affidavit and this order be served on the said Richard W. White at least three days before said last mentioned day.

W. SCULEY,
Judge Superior Court East. Dist. Ga.

January 22, 1869.

Filed this January 22, 1869.
GEO. WASHINGTON WILSON,
Deputy Clerk S. C. C. C.

SHERIFF'S OFFICE, }
CHATHAM COUNTY, January 22, 1869. }

I have this day served a copy of the within Petition, Affidavit and Order, personally, upon Richard W. White, the within named Defendant. The return of
ISAAC RUSSELL,
Deputy Clerk C. C.

CHATHAM COUNTY SUPERIOR COURT,

JANUARY TERM, 1869.

In Re, The Application of ⎫
WM. J. CLEMENTS, ⎪
For Leave to File Quo Warranto, ⎬
vs. ⎪
R. W. WHITE. ⎭

In the above matter it is declared that the Petition be granted, and that the Solicitor General of the Eastern District of Georgia do file an information in the nature of a Quo Warranto at the relation of Wm. J. Clements, calling on the said Richard W. White, acting as Clerk of the Superior Court of Chatham County, who is alleged to be a person of color, having in his veins one-eighth or more of African or negro blood, to show, twenty days after the service on him of a copy of said Quo Warranto, before the Judge of said Superior Court, at the Court House, at Savannah, at 10 A. M., by what warrant or right of law, he holds said office and discharges its duties and receives the emoluments thereof. Order granted February 4th, 1869.

CHATHAM SUPERIOR COURT,

STATE OF GEORGIA,
Ex Rel. Wm. J. Clements,
vs.
RICHARD W. WHITE.
    Quo Warranto.

In the above cause the Respondent having filed an answer raising an issue of facts, it is ordered that the same be tried by a Jury on the twenty-second day of March, 1869.
March 4th, 1869.

GEORGIA,
   CHATHAM COUNTY.

SUPERIOR COURT, JANUARY TERM, 1869.

Alfred B. Smith, Solicitor General of the Eastern Judicial District of Georgia, who sues for the State of Georgia, in this behalf, comes here into the Superior Court of Chatham County, in said Eastern Judicial District, before the Judge thereof, on the Fourth day of February, 1869, being in the January Term of said Court; and for the said State of Georgia, at the relation of William J. Clements, Esq., of said County and State, according to the law in such case made and provided, gives the Court here to understand and be informed, that at an election held in said County of Chatham, on the 21st, 22d, 23d and 24th days of April, 1868, for a Clerk of the Superior Court of the said County of Chatham, the said William J. Clements was the only eligible and qualified candidate who was voted for; that one Richard W. White, a person of color, having in his veins one-eighth or more of negro or African blood, received more votes than said Clements, but that White was and is ineligible to, and disqualified from holding, said office by reason of his being, as aforesaid, a person of color, having in his veins one-eighth or more of African or negro blood; and consequently, said Clements, being a white citizen, over the age of Twenty-one years, and eligible to, and qualified to hold, said office, is entitled to discharge its duties, exercise its powers and rights, receive the fees and emoluments arising from it, and to the occupation, custody and control of the offices, rooms, books, papers, and all other things connected with, or belonging to, said office; but that the said White for four months and more last past has used and exercised the said office of Clerk, discharged its duties, and received its fees and emoluments, to wit, in said County of Chatham, at the Court House, in the City of Savannah, and that the said White, a person of color, for and during all the time last above mentioned, without any legal warrant, grant or right whatsoever, at the City of Savannah, and in said County of Chatham, has claimed, and still does claim, to be the Clerk of the Superior Court of said County of Chatham, and to have, use and enjoy all the liberties, privileges and franchises to the office of said Clerk belonging and appertaining; which said office, with its liberties, privileges and franchises, he, the said Richard W. White, a person of color, has usurped and still doth usurp, at Savannah, in said County of Chatham, in contempt of said State of Georgia, and the people thereof, and to the damage and prejudices of said State, and also against its dignity.

ALFRED B. SMITH,
Solicitor General, Eastern Circuit of Georgia.
Filed February 12th, 1869.

Whereupon the Sheriff of Chatham County is commanded that he cause to come the said Richard W. White, acting as Clerk of said Superior Court of Chatham County, to answer by what warrant or authority he exercises the said office of Clerk of the Superior Court of Chatham County, at the Court House in Savannah, before the Judge of said Superior Court, twenty days after the service of a copy of this information and writ on him.

Witness the Honorable William Schley, Judge of said Superior Court of Chatham County, this February 12, 1869.

GEORGE WASHINGTON WILSON,
Deputy Clerk, S. C. C. C.

SHERIFF'S OFFICE,   }
CHATHAM COUNTY, February 12, 1869.   }

I have this day served a copy of the within paper personally upon Richard W. White. The return of

JAMES DOONER,
Sheriff Chatham County, Ga.

IN THE SUPERIOR COURT OF CHATHAM COUNTY.

JANUARY TERM, 1869.

THE STATE OF GEORGIA,
Ex Relatione,
WM. J. CLEMENTS,
vs.
RICHARD W. WHITE.

Information, Quo Warranto.

And now comes the said White, and not confessing or admitting any of the allegations in the said Information to be true, says that the matters and things contained are not sufficient in law, and that this Respondent is not bound to answer the same, and of this he prays the judgment of the Court.

A. W. STONE,
J. JOHNSON,
Attorneys for Respondent.

Demurrer filed March 4th, 1869.
GEORGE WASHINGTON WILSON,
Deputy Clerk, S. C. C. C.

The foregoing demurrer was withdrawn on the day it was filed. No argument was ever had upon it. The Defendant moved for a continuance upon the demurrer, because of the absence of associate counsel. The Court refused the continuance, because leading counsel was present; whereupon Defendant withdrew the demurrer and filed an issuable plea or answer, upon which he did obtain the continuance. A Jury was then drawn to try the issue.

W. SCHLEY,
Judge Superior Court East. Dist. Ga.

STATE OF GEORGIA,
Ex Relatione,
WM. J. CLEMENTS,
vs.
RICHARD W. WHITE,
Clerk of Superior Court of Chatham Co.

Quo Warranto.
In Chatham Superior Court.

The Writ of *Quo Warranto* alleges that the Respondent,

Richard W. White, is a person of color, having one-eighth of negro or African blood in his veins, and that he is, for that reason, disqualified to hold the office of Clerk of the Superior Court, the functions of which he is now discharging.

The Respondent demurs to the sufficiency of this ground in law, and I am called upon to decide the question of Respondent's eligibility to office in Georgia. In other words, the question is, can a negro hold office in Georgia?

It is admitted by Counsel for the Respondent that previous to the adoption of the negro by our State and Federal Governments as a citizen, he was ineligible to office. This proposition is so clear that it does not admit of argument. But it may be well to consider the status of the negro up to the adoption of our present State Constitution, in order to assist us in ascertaining his present condition. The negro, excepting the few free persons of color in Georgia up to the close of the late war, was that of a chattel. He had no State relations—the master was the citizen—the negro was his subject. The law recognized him by protecting his life and limb, but no further. He had no political right of any imaginable nature. The State and Federal Constitutions treated him as a slave. He was neither citizen, denizen, nor alien, but bore in his name and race every political disability. And such he remained at the time of general emancipation. The first step taken for his relief was to give him freedom by an Ordinance of this State in Convention assembled in 1865. The next step was to enable him to sue, testify, and acquire and hold property and money. And these were all the privileges conferred upon him until the adoption of our present State Constitution, and of the 14th Amendment to the Federal Constitution. And as the language of the 14th Amendment, and of our Constitution, in conferring citizenship on the negro is the same, the grant in the latter, if differing at all, being broader than the former, I shall consider them both together.

And first, I will say so far as the rights conferred by citizenship are concerned, the 14th Amendment was as ample as the 2d Section of the 1st Article of our State Constitution. Both declare all persons born in the United States and resident in Georgia to be citizens of Georgia, and both guarantee "all the privileges and immunities of citizens of the United States," and of this State. If, therefore, citizenship *ipso facto* or *ex vi termini* does not confer the right to hold office, as the Federal Constitution grants nothing more than the privileges and immunities of citizenship, we will have to look further into our State Constitution to see whether the rights of office is therein given to this class of citizens. It must be borne in mind that we are now considering only the privileges and immunities of citizenship, which are conferred alike by the Federal and State Constitutions. And to estimate properly the effect of this grant, let us suppose that the 2d Section, 1st Article of our State Constitution had been omitted. Would not every privilege and immunity conferred by our Constitution in said 2d Section have been as complete as they are now? Certainly, because the 14th Amendment being a part of the Federal Constitution, which is the supreme law, not only becomes a part of our State Constitution so to speak, but it controls it, so that it was as unnecessary to repeat the language of the 14th Amendment in our Constitution as to have said that no law should be passed impairing the obligation of a contract, or that no *ex post facto* law should be enacted.

This being settled, we are now prepared to inquire into the extent of the privileges and immunities of citizenship in Georgia, as conferred by the 14th amendment. In other words, we must inquire what privileges and immunities the Federal Constitution and Government can confer on a citizen of Georgia. I answer, considering the question negatively, that the power to confer the elective franchise and eligibility to a State office is not vested in the Federal Government, or embraced in the Federal Constitution. These are reserved State's rights; the elective franchise is controlled by each State. Any State can confer it on its citizens, or on denizens or temporary inhabitants, or on aliens. Any State can establish a property qualification, or an intelligence qualification, or a qualification based on class or race. Again: any State can make eligible to office certain of her citizens, and exclude all others, or can give office to aliens, minors, women, negroes, or Indians. Over these questions the Federal Government has no control. Hence, we see the effort being made now to so amend the Federal Constitution as to confer on all citizens the right to vote. If the Federal Government, under the Constitution, could not before or since the adoption of the 14th amendment, confer on the citizens of any State the elective franchise and the right to hold a State office, or either, it must follow that neither of these rights has been conferred on the citizens of Georgia, white or colored, unless they are included in the meaning of the words "privileges and immunities of citizenship of the United States, or of this State." This brings us to consider, first, whether the right to vote and eligibility to office are, or either is, embraced in the privileges and immunities of a citizen of a State; and if not, then, secondly, whether those rights, by the laws of Georgia in force at the adoption of our present Constitution, were incidents to citizenship in Georgia. On the first point we are fortified by abundant authority, to the effect that citizenship embraces neither of these two rights. The question is settled beyond a doubt by the State and Federal Courts. In Dred Scott *vs.* Sandford, 19 How. 422, Chief Justice Taney says, with emphasis, "undoubtedly, a person may be a citizen, that is, a member of the community who form the sovereignty, although he exercises no show of the political power, and is incapacitated from holding particular offices; women and minors, who form a part of the political family, cannot vote; and when a property qualification is required to vote or hold a particular office, those who have not the necessary qualification cannot vote or hold the office, yet they are citizens."

Again: in a very recent case decided by Justice Swayne, of the United States Supreme Court, as Circuit Judge in Kentucky, and reported in full in the Law Register of February last, that Judge says: "Citizenship has no necessary connection with the franchise of voting, eligibility to office, or, indeed, with any other right, civil or political; women, minors, and persons non-compos, are citizens, and not the less so on account of their disabilities." Again: "The fact that one is a subject or citizen determines nothing as to his rights as such: they vary in different localities, and according to circumstances." In the State *vs.* Manuel, 4 Dev. & Batt. 26, Judge Gaston says: "The term citizen, as understood in our law, is precisely analagous to the term *subject* in the common law, and the change of phrase has entirely resulted from the change of government. The sovereignty has been changed from one man to the collective body of the people, and he who before *was a subject of the King*, is now a *citizen of the State*." Again: Mr. Justice Curtis, in his dissenting opinion delivered in the Dred Scott case, page 583, says: "So in all the States, numerous persons, though citizens, cannot vote, or cannot hold office, either on account of their age or sex, or the want of the necessary legal qualifications. The truth is that citizenship, under the Constitution of the United States, is not dependent on the possession of any particular political, or even of all civil rights, and any attempt so to define it must lead to error. To what citizens the elective franchise shall be confided is a question to be determined by each State, in accordance with its own views of the necessities or expediencies of its condition. What civil rights shall be enjoyed by its citizens, and whether all shall enjoy the same, or how they may be gained or lost, are to be determined in the same way." Again: in Wash. C. C. Reps., vol. 4, page 381, Corfield *vs.* Coryell, Judge Washington says: "The inquiry is, what are the privileges and immunities of citizens in the several States? We feel no hesitation in confining these expressions to those privileges and immunities which are in their nature *fundamental*, which belong right to the citizens of all free Government, and which have at all times been enjoyed by the citizens of the several States which compose this Union, from the time of their becoming free, independent and sovereign. What these fundamental principles are, it would perhaps be more tedious than difficult to enumerate. They may, however, be all comprehended under the following general heads: protection by the Government, the enjoyment of life and liberty, with the right to acquire and possess property of every kind, and to pursue and obtain happiness and safety, subject, nevertheless, to such restraints as the Government may justly prescribe for the general good of the whole.

"The right of a citizen of one State to pass through or to reside in any other State, for purposes of trade, agriculture, professional pursuits, or otherwise; to claim the benefit of the writ of *habeas corpus*; to institute and maintain actions of any kind in the courts of the State, to take hold of and dispose of property, either real or personal, and an exemption from higher taxes or impositions than are paid by the other citizens of the State, may be mentioned as some of the particular privileges and immunities of citizens, which are clearly embraced by the general description of privileges deemed to be fundamental, to which may be added the elective franchise, as regulated and established by the laws or Constitution of the State in which it is to be exercised."

If, then, as we have thus seen, the right to vote and to hold office are not included in the grant of citizenship, if they are not necessarily among the privileges and immunities, which belong to every citizen, and which cannot be abridged, but, as Justice Washington, Swayne, Curtis, and Chief Justice Taney declare, to be regulated by the laws or Constitution of the State in which they are to be exercised; we must look to our State Constitution and State laws for the true solution of this question; by them, and them only, we must be governed.

I have already said that the 14th amendment would have

been as effectual in securing the rights of a citizen of Georgia as the 2d section of the first article of our State Constitution; I mean by that to say that if the elective franchise or eligibility to office in Georgia depended on the said section alone—that is, if the remainder of the Constitution and the State laws were silent as to either of these rights—the said second section could have been omitted without detriment to any citizen's rights in Georgia; and I have stated that the 14th amendment did not confer either the right to vote or eligibility to office. This conclusion may be doubted, and I will therefore notice that point still further. Let us compare the two and see if they vary in meaning. The 14th amendment is: "All persons born or naturalized in the United States, and subject to the jurisdiction thereof, are citizens of the United States and of the State wherein they reside. No State shall make or enforce any law which shall abridge the privileges or immunities of citizens of the United States; nor shall any State deprive any person of life, liberty or property without due process of law, nor deny to any person within its jurisdiction the equal protection of the laws," The State Constitution reads: "All persons born and naturalized in the United States, and resident in this State, are hereby declared citizens of this State, and no laws shall be made or enforced which shall abridge the privileges or immunities of citizens of the United States or of this State, or deny to any person within its jurisdiction the equal protection of its laws. And it shall be the duty of the General Assembly, by appropriate legislation, to protect every person in the due enjoyment of the rights, privileges and immunities guaranteed in this section." The clause in the amendment about life, liberty, &c., is surplusage, as it was already in the Constitution. The only imaginable difference is in the fact that the amendment forbids the abridgement of the privileges or immunities of "citizens of the United States," while our Constitution says of " citizens of the United States, *or of this State.*" But the language in both relates, as we have seen, upon authority not to *political*, but to *personal* rights of citizens. But the respondent insists that the right to vote and eligibility to office are included in those words. I will concede that if before and at the time of the adoption of our Constitution *all citizens* had the right to vote and to hold office, there would be much force in this position; for all persons born and naturalized in the United States, and resident in Georgia at that time, were declared to be citizens, and the privileges and immunities of all such citizens are thereby guaranteed, and cannot be abridged. But just here the *onus* lies upon the respondent to show that *all* citizens of Georgia could, before and at that time, vote and hold office. The position cannot be evaded. The privileges and immunities referred to belong to all citizens of this State. They were such as were common to each and every citizen. If the respondent deny this position, his right to office, so far as it depends in this second section of the Constitution, has no foundation. If he admits it, then he must take its logical consequences; for by that section *all persons* (white and colored, male and female,) were declared to be citizens of Georgia, and it is "the rights, privileges and immunities of *all* citizens" which are guaranteed, and which cannot be abridged. Then it follows, as a necessary consequence, that either the right to vote and eligibility to office were not conferred on any persons or class of persons by that section, or that they were conferred on all persons and classes who were thereby declared to be citizens. But this section makes women and children citizens, and if the right to vote and hold office was thereby given to any persons, women and children have the right to vote and are eligible to office. This conclusion is inevitable—if it once be granted that the Convention intended to confer, and did confer, the franchise of voting and of office by the use of the words "rights, privileges and immunities." But we must now see if any other portion of our Constitution gives to colored citizens the right to hold office. It is urged that this right is given by the 2d clause, 2d section, Article III, which is in these words: "The Senators shall be citizens of the United States who have attained the age of twenty-five years, and who, after the first election under this Constitution, shall have been citizens of this State for two years, and for one year resident of the District from which elected." It is insisted that no other qualification is required for one to be a Senator. This proceeds upon the assumption that the Convention intended that every citizen having those qualifications could be a Senator. This, it seems to me, is strange logic, that the effect would have been to make voters of women, white and colored, as well as of males. But it would not have followed that every woman, white and colored, would thereby have been eligible to office. The former does not include the latter. The latter is a higher political right. It presupposes qualifications superior to those fitting a person to vote, just as it requires other and higher qualifications to be a voter than to be a citizen. There is a gradation in these relations to the State, and while eligibility to office presupposes the right to vote, and voting presupposes citizenship—as the one ordinarily precedes the other—on the other hand, citizenship does not include the elective franchise, nor the elective franchise the right to hold office, any more than the less includes the greater. Eligibility to office for the male negro is not, therefore, to be *inferred* from the clause which clothes him with the elective franchise. That I am right in this, not only on principle, but on the letter of the clause itself, will appear more clearly when we consider the fact, that if that clause conferred the further right to hold office on the male negro, it also conferred the same right on aliens. For it reads, "Every *male person* born in the United States, and every *male person* who has been naturalized, *or who has legally declared his intention to become a citizen* of the United States, twenty-one years old, &c., shall be deemed an elector." Certainly, the Convention did not intend to throw the offices of the State into the hands of aliens.

But if the male negro citizen is, by the above clause, advanced to the highest political rights, to wit: eligibility to office, the male person who simply declares his intention to become a citizen, (and who may never carry out that intention,) is also clothed with the same right. This is an inference not to be lightly made. We should and must require unmistakable language in this case likewise, to justify such a construction as would place our State offices in the hands of aliens. This would, however, be the effect, because there is no provision in our Constitution requiring citizenship as a qualification to eligibility to office in one out of ten of the many State offices.

And if the Constitution thus confers the right to office on an alien, it must be borne in mind that the Legislature is powerless to prescribe citizenship as a qualification. And hence it would follow that any alien, a Congo, an Ebo, a Hottentot, fresh from his jungles, who should declare his intention to become a citizen, would be clothed with the highest political right known to our people, after six months residence in Georgia.

This disposes of the provisions of the Constitution bearing upon this question, and we are brought, finally, to the statute laws of Georgia; do they confer on the colored citizen the right to hold office? The Code which was adopted by the Constitution as law, divides the natural persons of Georgia into four classes—citizens, residents not citizens, aliens, and persons of color. It says that among the rights of citizens are the elective franchise and the right to hold office. And as the Constitution has made persons of color citizens,

it is insisted, as a necessary consequence, that they have all
the rights which were given to citizens as they were defined
when the Code was passed, and afterward adopted by the
Convention. But we have seen that persons of color, before
the adoption of the Code, had no political rights. We have
seen, also, that political rights are not conferred by implication of law, and that the removal of one disability does not
include the removal of any other, unless the one removed
be the greater. Citizenship was first conferred; that did
not remove necessarily the disability as to the elective franchise, for if it did so for the person of color, who, by the classification given above, ranks lower in the State than white
females, who are citizens, it must *a fortiori*, have removed the
disability from all females. If declaring the negro to be a citizen made him a citizen in the sense intended in the Code, all
females and all minors are likewise clothed with the elective
franchise and the right to hold office. If they are not, then
the Constitution, by making persons of color citizens, elevated them above white females and minors. But will it be
pretended that females can vote and hold office in Georgia?
Can the conclusion be avoided, however, if the monstrous construction be put upon the Code, whereby the lowest class of
natural persons, and who rested under *every* disability before
the Constitution was adopted, are relieved of all disabilities
by the grant of mere citizenship, the want of which was the
least of his disabilities. If the Convention intended to give
this construction, why did they by positive enactment go
one step further and confer the right to vote on persons of
color? If citizenship gave the right, why confer it in express terms? If the Constitution considered that the right
to hold office was conferred by the Code as incident to citizenship, why was not the right to vote also so considered?
And if so, why expressly confer the less right, and remain
silent as to the greater right? If the Convention had given
in express terms the right to hold office, the silence as to the
elective franchise would have been proper, not to say logical, because the right to hold office necessarily comes with
it the right to vote. I can put no other construction on this
action of the Convention than that they meant to give only
such rights as are given in express terms. And this conclusion is made certain by the record of their proceedings,
which shows that they by solemn vote rejected the amendment which was offered to give the right to hold office to
persons of color. If, then, we are to be controlled by the
express grant of political rights in our Constitution to per-

sons of color, the right to hold office in Georgia does not belong to any person of color.

The Demurrer is therefore overruled.

WM. SCHLEY,
Judge Superior Court, Eastern Circuit Georgia.

———

CHATHAM SUPERIOR COURT,

JANUARY TERM, 1869.

THE STATE, ex Relatione,
vs.
R. W. WHITE.

And now at this Term comes the said Defendant, and for answer to the complaint aforesaid, says : That at the election held in said County, on the 21st, 22d, 23d and 24th of April, 1868, for Clerk of the Superior Court of said County, he was a candidate, and that at said election he received a majority of all the votes cast or polled ; that he was then, had been, and now is a citizen of the United States and of the State of Georgia, and County of Chatham ; that he was and is eligible and qualified by law for said office, and being so eligible and qualified and elected as aforesaid afterwards, to-wit, on the seventh day of August, 1868, he was duly commissioned as Clerk of said Court by the Governor of the State of Georgia, and thereupon entered upon the discharge of the duties of said office, and has in his possession as such Clerk the books and papers pertaining to said office. And this Defendant for further answer says that he is not a person of color, nor does he have in his veins one-eighth or more of negro or African blood.

Wherefore this Defendant says that he is not guilty of usurping said office, as thereof alleged against him, and prays the judgment of the Court.

A. W. STONE and J. JOHNSON,
Respondent's Attorneys.

Personally appeared before me, Richard W. White, who,

2

being duly sworn, says the facts stated in the foregoing answer are true.

RICHARD W. WHITE.

Subscribed and sworn to before me {
March 4th, 1869.   }
W. SCHLEY,
Judge Superior Court Eastern Circuit Ga.

Answer filed March 4th, 1869.
GEORGE WASHINGTON WILSON,
Deputy Clerk S. C. C. C.

VERDICT.

We, the Jury, find that the Defendant has one-eighth African blood in his veins, and is a colored man under the laws of Georgia.

ISAAC D. LAROCHE, Foreman.

The foregoing answer had been filed before the argument was had upon which I based my decision for the conclusion given to counsel for Relator, and was the only papers filed by Defendant in the case, the original demurrer having been withdrawn.   W. SCHLEY,
Judge Superior Court Eastern Circuit, Ga.

———

STATE OF GEORGIA, ⎫
Ex Relatione,   ⎪
W. J. CLEMENTS,   ⎬   *Quo Warranto.*
vs.   ⎪
RICHARD WHITE. ⎭

And hereupon all and singular the premises being seen and fully understood by the Court here, and the said Court having considered and adjudged the Exceptions and Demurrer of the said Respondent to be insufficient in law, and all and particular the matters above put in issue having been tried by the country; and the Jury having determined by the verdict as follows: "We, the Jury, find the Defendant has one-eighth of African blood in his veins, and is a colored man under the laws of Georgia." And it appearing to the Court by its said decision on the law, and the said verdict of the Jury on the facts put in issue, that the said Respondent, Richard W. White, hath usurped, and still doth usurp, the place, office liberties, privileges and franchises of Clerk of the Superior Court of the County of Chatham, in manner and form, as in and by the above information is charged against him; therefore, it is considered and ordered by the said Court here, that the said Richard W. White, a person of color, do not in any manner intermeddle with or concern himself in and about the office, liberties, privileges and franchises aforesaid, but that he be absolutely forejudged and excluded from ever exercising or using the same or any of them for the future; and that the said William J. Clements, the Relator above mentioned in this behalf do recover against the said Richard W. White the sum of six dollars and fifty cents for his costs by him laid out and expended in carrying on his suit in this behalf according to the law in such case made and provided.

W. Schley,
Judge Superior Court Eastern Circuit Ga.

April 1st, 1869.

A. B. Smith, Solicitor General.

J. Hartridge, }
T. E. Lloyd, } Attorneys for Relator.
W. B. Fleming, }

Judgment entered up and signed and filed this April 1st, 1869.

George Washington Wilson,
Deputy Clerk S. C. C. C.

IN THE SUPREME COURT OF GEORGIA.

June Term, 1869.

BILL OF EXCEPTIONS.

Georgia—Chatham County.

The State of Georgia,
Ex Relatione,
W. J. Clements,
vs.
Richard W. White.

Be it remembered that said cause came on to be tried in said County on the twenty-second day of March, 1869, under an order of said Court; that on said day said Defendant appeared and filed a Demurrer and Answer to said Information, and also filed a written Affidavit, and upon said affidavit moved the Court for a continuance of said cause. The said Court, upon consideration, overruled the motion to continue the case, and thereupon the Defendant then and now excepts to said ruling of the Court, and assigns the same for Error. A copy of said affidavit is annexed and marked (A). The Defendant then presented said Demurrer or Exception filed by him, a copy of which is annexed marked (B), and insisted he had the right to open and conclude the argument on the Demurrer. The Court, upon consideration, ruled that the Plaintiff had the right to open and conclude said argument and so allowed said Plaintiff; and thereupon the Defendant then and now excepts and assigns said ruling for Error. The reason was this: the Counsel for the Defendant had already put in a Demurrer to the application for Quo Warranto, and withdrawn it. He had filed an Answer and prayed an issue; he had moved for a continuance upon the issue made by his Answer, which continuance was refused. Defendant's Counsel then called up his Demurrer or Exception, which would properly have been heard after the verdict upon the issue, as the Answer suspended, if it did not overrule the Demurrer. The Counsel for the Relator—whilst not objecting to the argument of the legal point at that time—insisted that as the Demurrer had been originally withdrawn and an Answer had been filed, and that the argument asked for by Counsel for the Defendant was to settle all the legal questions in the case that the Relator as the promovent in the case was entitled to the conclusion of the argument.

The argument on the Demurrer having been concluded the Court overruled the Demurrer, deciding that under the Constitution and Laws of Georgia a person of color was ineligible to office. To which decision of the Court overruling the Demurrer, the Defendant then and now excepts and assigns the same for Error.

A jury then came to try the issue between the parties, and the Plaintiff introduced several witnesses, whose names and testimony are hereto annexed, marked (D). To so much of the testimony of Albert Jackson as related to his acts as Register, and to so much as related to the reputation of Defendant being a man of color, the Defendant objected. The Court overruled the objections and allowed the testimony to be submitted to the Jury. To which ruling of the Court last aforesaid said Defendant then and now excepts and assigns the same for Error.

To so much of the testimony of Dr. Young, as is founded on his medical knowledge, and his opinion as such, the Defendant objected. The Court overruled the objection and allowed the same to be submitted to the Jury. To which said ruling the Defendant then and now excepts and assigns the same for Error.

The Plaintiff introduced the witness, Howard, who testified that a certain book was a Record Book of an Insurance Company, that had recorded in it an application for a Policy from R. W. White; that the original application had, after record, been sent to New York where it then was; that the original was truly copied in said book; that he did not know who presented said application; that he did not see Defendant sign it, nor did he know Defendant's hand writing. The Plaintiff offered to read said copy in said Insurance Book in evidence, and the Defendant objected. The Court overruled the objection and allowed said copy in said book to be read in evidence, and thereupon the Defendant then and now excepts and assigns the same for Error. A copy of the copy is annexed, marked E.

The Plaintiff here closed; the Defendant offered no testimony, and after argument had the Defendant requested the Court to charge the Jury that the Defendant being in the exercise of the functions of the office, the presumption of the law is that he is entitled to it, and it is incumbent on the

Plaintiff to rebut such presumption by legal proof, and if Plaintiff should fail to make out every point in his case they must find for the Defendant; which charge the Court refused to give, but charged the Jury that—

First—The Law says any person having one-eighth or more of negro or African blood in his veins is ineligible to office; I have, therefore, decided on the Demurrer that a negro or person of color cannot hold office in Georgia.

Second—The legal question then having been disposed of by the Court, the issue of fact is now submitted for your consideration, whether or not the Defendant has one-eighth of negro or African blood in his veins.

Third—You must now look to the testimony and see if the Plaintiff has legally proven to your satisfaction, that the Defendant has one-eighth of negro or African blood in his veins. If he has not, then, you must find for the Defendant, but if it is proven to your satisfaction that the Defendant has the one-eighth or more of negro or African blood in his veins, then you cannot but find for the Plaintiff.

Fourth—In this case the Respondent dwells upon the insufficiency of the Relator's proof, and asks at your hands a verdict in his favor.

Fifth—I am requested to charge you on the character of the testimony—that where blood, race, &c., is the subject—that you can take general hearsay, or the reputation of the person in his community, that is what he says of himself—what others say of him—his associates, and his general reputation as such in the community in which he resides, &c., in order to determine as to his being a white man, or a person of color. Under slavery no records were kept of Births or Marriages among slaves, and hence the rule as to general reputation and hearsay was more applicable to blacks than to whites. Now you must look to the testimony and be satisfied in your minds that the facts disclose one-eighth or more of negro or African blood in the veins of the Respondent before you can find for the Relator. I am further requested by the Defendant to charge you "that the Defendant being in the exercise of the functions of the office, the presumption of the law is that he is entitled to the office, and it is incumbent on the Plaintiff to rebut such presumption by legal proof, and if the Plaintiff should fail to make out every point in his case, you must find for the Defendant." I cannot charge you in the language asked for, but I do charge you as a general principle of law, that any person holding an office, the law presumes him eligible and competent to hold the same, but that presumption refers to his acts as such officer where the rights of others were affected, such as attestation, and other acts in the line of his office. But where, as in this case, the issue had no reference to any official act, but as to the race or blood of the Defendant, disqualifying him from holding office, there was *not* such a presumption of law as contemplated by the language contained in the request to charge. But that the law, in this issue, did not make the presumption as contended for by Defendant's Counsel—that the Jury must look to the testimony submitted to them and determine the case from the proofs. I am further requested to charge you, that if the Plaintiff fails to make out his case in every point they must find for the Defendant. I cannot charge you in these words, but I do charge that you must be satisfied, from the testimony before you, that the Defendant has one-eighth or more of negro or African blood in his veins, before you can find for the Plaintiff.

To the refusal of the Court to charge as requested, and to the charge as given, the Defendant then and now excepts and assigns the same for Error.

For as much as the matters and things aforesaid do not appear of record, the said Defendant within thirty days from the time of making said decisions, presents this his Bill of Exceptions, and prays the same may be signed and certified and made a part of the Record in said Cause.

A. W. STONE,
JAMES JOHNSON,
Respondent's Attorneys.

April 2, 1869.

SAVANNAH, GEORGIA, Chatham County, }
April 12th, 1869. }

We acknowledge due and legal service of this Bill of Exceptions and the receipt of a copy thereof.

ALFRED B. SMITH, Solicitor General.
THOS. E. LLOYD, Sol. for Relator.
JULIAN HARTRIDGE, Sol. for Relator.

(A)

THE STATE, ex Relatione,
WM. J. CLEMENTS,
vs.
R. W. WHITE.

Quo Warranto, in the Superior Court of Chatham County.

The Defendant, Richard W. White, moves the Court for a continuance in the above stated cause, and for cause of continuance says: That on the 6th day of March, 1869, he, by his counsel, A. W. Stone, prepared a set of interrogatories to be propounded to Charles Green, a material witness for the Respondent, and who resides in San Francisco, California; that on the same day he was informed by his said counsel that the said interrogatories had been handed to or left at the office of Hartridge & Chisholm, counsel for Relator; that on the Monday following the interrogatories were returned crossed to his said counsel, and by him deposited, properly stamped, in the post office, in Savannah, directed to Edward Everett, one of the commissioners named in the commission, to be executed and returned. That the said interrogatories have not been returned; that the witness resides in San Francisco, California, and over five hundred miles from Savannah; that the testimony of the said witness is material to his defense; that by said witness he expects to prove his race and nationality, and that there is no negro or African blood in his veins. That deponent expects the said interrogatories will be executed and returned to said Court within the time limited by the rules of Court for the return of commissions of a witness more than five hundred miles from the place of trial, and that he will be able to procure such testimony by the next term of said Court. That the said cause was assigned on the fourth of March for trial on the twenty-second; that the interrogatories were made out and handed to counsel for Relator on the sixth, and mailed on the eighth of March. Deponent submits to the Court if he has not shown due diligence in suing out and having had said interrogatories executed.

Sworn to and subscribed before me this, the twenty-second day of March, A. D., 1869.

RICHARD W. WHITE.

PHILIP M. RUSSELL, JR.,
Notary Public and ex-officio Justice of the Peace, Chatham County, State of Georgia.

(B)

IN THE SUPERIOR COURT OF CHATHAM COUNTY.

JANUARY TERM, 1869.

THE STATE OF GEORGIA,
Ex Relatione,
vs.
RICHARD W. WHITE. }

Information, Quo Warranto.

And now comes the said White, and not confessing or admitting any of the allegations in the said information to be true, says: That the matters and things therein contained are not sufficient in law, and that this Respondent is not bound to answer the same, and of this he prays the judgment of the Court.

A. W. STONE,
J. JOHNSON,
Attorneys for Respondent.

(D)

Richard Mimms, p. c., sworn, and says: "I met Richard W. White some time since in Captain Doyle's store, either last summer or the summer before last; he told me that he, White, came from Barnwell District before the war; he made his escape from a master or a guardian. I do not recollect the language White used. I do not know the distance from Barnwell District. I was never there. I am from Edgefield, South Carolina, myself. White and I had a difficulty some time ago; we have not spoke, but I have nothing against him at this time. That he, White, came from South Carolina originally."

A. N. Wilson sworn, and says: "I know this Respondent. The first time I ever saw him was in October or November, 1867, in a meeting which was held for the purpose of nominating candidates for the State Constitutional Convention. White made a speech (the first, I think,) in favor of nominating an equal number of whites and blacks; that is, in behalf of the colored part of the Convention, when I inquired and found out his name."

Albert Jackson sworn, and says: " I was one of the Registers in the year 1867. There was a check put after White's name to designate him as a colored man. A list designating persons which had been arranged by the Board was posted up at the Court House. I do not know whether or not it was there all the time during the election. From these facts, and seeing him several times in the company of colored persons, I took him to be one. I have seen Spaniards and Italians as dark as White. I believe White is reputed a person of color. That the list of the registered voters was put up in the Court House for two or three weeks before the election. That against the name of the defendant the letter C. was marked, indicating colored. The Registers left the list open for correction for three weeks before the election, and that White did not ask any correction."

Dr. Easton Yonge sworn, and says: " I have been a practicing physician for twenty years ; examined the respondent and gave a certificate to the Knickerbocker Insurance Company as a mulatto. I have studied the science of Ethnology, but not a great deal. This study leads one to inquire the difference of races. I came to the conclusion, however, that respondent was a mulatto from external indications. I think any intelligent person could tell as well as I could, (if much among the negroes,) the difference between a white man and a person of color, from observation."

J. S. Howard sworn, and says : "This book in Court contains copies of all applications for life insurance to the Knickerbocker Life Insurance Company. The originals are all sent on to New York. This application, which is signed with the name of respondent, I think was signed by himself for his wife. I do not know his hand-writing ; don't know whether he or his wife signed the name."

GEORGIA,
   Chatham County. }

I do certify that the foregoing Bill of Exceptions is true, and contains all the evidence material to a clear understanding of the errors complained of, and the Deputy Clerk of the Superior Court of the county of Chatham, is hereby required and ordered to make out a complete copy of the record of said case, and certify the same as such, and cause the same to be transmitted to the Supreme Court at the June Term, on the first Monday thereof, at Atlanta, in the year

1869, that the errors alleged to have been committed may be considered and corrected.

Given under my hand and seal this the sixth day of April, A. D., 1869, and within thirty days of the making said decisions.

I respectfully refer the Court to my explanation at bottom of page containing Demurrer, and bottom of page containing the Answer or issuable plea. } W. SCHLEY, [L. S.]

Judge Sup. Court,
East'n Circuit, Ga.

GEORGIA,
   CHATHAM COUNTY. }

I. Georgia W. Wilson, Deputy Clerk of the Superior Court of the county of Chatham, in the State aforesaid, do hereby certify that the foregoing is a true and complete transcript of the record in the case of "The State of Georgia *ex relatione* William J. Clements *versus* Richard W. White, Clerk Superior Court, Chatham County," *Quo Warranto,* and the original Bill of Exceptions, a copy of which is on file in this office. And I do further certify that the Respondent has paid all costs, and filed his bond, with good security, in terms of the law.

In testimony whereof, I have hereunto set my official signature and seal of office, at Savannah, this the seventh day of April, Anno Domini, One Thousand Eight Hundred and Sixty-nine.

GEO. WASHINGTON WILSON,
Dep. Clerk S. C. C. C.

————

At the conclusion of the reading of the record, the hour of six o'clock, P. M., having arrived, the Court adjourned until ten o'clock to-morrow morning, the 10th instant.

ATLANTA, GA., June 10, 1869.

The Court opened at 10 o'clock, A. M. His Honor the Chief Justice, presiding.

ARGUMENT OF COL. STONE.

COL. A. W. STONE opened the argument for the Plaintiff in Error. He said:

MAY IT PLEASE THE COURT: Before entering into the argument upon the merits of this case, I desire to remark how unnecessary and, to my mind, reprehensible, is the practice adopted in our Circuit, by our Judge, of sending up to this Court, as part of the record of the Court below, a lengthy decision, like that which is attached to this case.

I have no objection to a Judge of the Superior Court making an argument in this Court on any case he pleases, but I should prefer his doing so at his own expense, rather than at that of my client or myself.

I just make this remark for the ear of the Court, as it will be seen that the argument of the learned Judge below, in this case, occupies more of the record brought before this Court than the Bill of Exceptions and the balance of the record.

The Court will have observed that there are several points made in this Bill of Exceptions to which I shall briefly call your Honors' attention.

It seems to me that the Errors of the Judge below are so plain that no arguments are necessary to convince this Court of the fact. And I only introduce them, and use them here, for the purpose of showing what surrounded us in the trial of this case in the Court below—with the feelings and prejudices of the whole community opposed to us. Not a single point that was raised by the learned counsel for the Defendant in Error here—the Plaintiff below—was ruled in our favor.

The first question is on the motion for continuance—the overruling of that motion.

It will be borne in mind that we filed a demurrer, and also an answer, denying that Mr. White was a person of color. That raising an issue of fact, when the case was called for a hearing we moved for a continuance, and the affidavit I will read to the Court:

"THE STATE, ex Relatione, ⎫
    WM. J. CLEMENTS, ⎪   Quo Warranto, in the Superior
        vs. ⎬   Court of Chatham County.
    R. W. WHITE. ⎭

The Defendant, Richard W. White, moves the Court for
a continuance in the above stated cause, and for cause of
continuance says : That on the 6th day of March, 1869, he,
by his counsel, A. W. Stone, prepared a set of interrogatories to be propounded to Charles Green, a material witness
for the Respondent, and who resides in San Francisco, California ; that on the same day he was informed by his said
counsel that the said interrogatories had been handed to, or
left at the office of, Hartridge & Chisholm, counsel for Relator ; that on the Monday following the interrogatories
were returned crossed to his said counsel, and by him deposited, properly stamped, in the post office, in Savannah,
directed to Edward Everett, one of the commissioners named
in the commission, to be executed and returned. That the
said interrogatories have not been returned ; that the witness resides in San Francisco, California, and over five hundred miles from Savannah ; that the testimony of the said
witness is material to his defense ; that by said witness he
expects to prove his race and nationality, and that there is
no negro or African blood in his veins. That deponent expects the said interrogatories will be executed and returned to
said Court within the time limited by the rules of Court for
the return of commissions of a witness more than five hundred
miles from the place of trial, and that he will be able to
procure such testimony by the next term of said Court.
That the said cause was assigned on the fourth of March,
for trial on the twenty-second ; that the interrogatories were
made out and handed to counsel for Relator on the sixth,
and mailed on the eighth of March. Deponent submits to
the Court if he has not shown due diligence in sueing out
and having had said interrogatories executed.

    Sworn to and subscribed before ⎫
me this, the twenty-second day of ⎬   RICHARD W. WHITE.
March, A. D., 1869. ⎭
    PHILIP M. RUSSELL, JR.,
Notary Public and ex-officio Justice of the Peace, Chatham
  County, Georgia."

The case was assigned on the 4th of March for trial on
the 22d of the same month. Interrogatories were made out
the next day and forwarded to the proper parties in due

course of mail ; and only eighteen days had elapsed from the time of suing out the commission until the time of trial. The time had not expired for the return of the commission of a witness residing more than five hundred miles from the city of Savannah.

I call your Honors' attention to the 3478th Section of the Code, in connection with the 3471st :

"§ 3478. When a commission issues to examine a witness, it not having been returned shall be no cause of a continuance unless the party seeking the continuance will make the same oath of the materiality of the testimony as in the case of an absent witness; and the party must show due diligence in suing out and having the same executed."

Your Honors will observe that the Code only prescribes that we shall make the same oath as to the materiality of the testimony as in the case of an absent witness, and show due diligence. What is the rule in this connection in regard to an absent witness? I will read the 3471st Section of the Code on that subject :

"In all applications for continuances upon the ground of the absence of a witness, it must be shown to the Court that that the witness is absent; that he has been subpœnaed; that he resides in the county where the case is pending; that his testimony is material ; that such witness is not absent by the permission, directly or indirectly, of such applicant; that he expects he will be able to procure the testimony of such absent witness at the next term of the Court ; and that such application is not made for the purpose of delay, but to enable the party to procure the testimony of such absent witness, and must state the facts expected to be proven by such absent witness."

The materiality of the testimony exists in the statement of facts which we expected to prove by the absent witness. What were these facts? That the defendant, White, was not a person of color—that he had no negro or African blood in his veins. We so stated in our affidavit; we so stated to the Court. Yet the motion for a continuance was overruled. If that affidavit is held insufficient I am at a loss to conceive how a party asking a continuance on account of the absence of interrogatories, can ever make a showing. We had literally and fully complied with the language of the Code, and yet our motion for a continuance was peremptorily and absolutely refused.

The next Error, may it please your Honors, is upon the ruling of the Court in regard to the demurrer. The Court ruled in this case that the Relator had the right to open and conclude the argument on the demurrer. This is, in my opinion, the first time in the history of the jurisprudence of Georgia when a Judge has held that the party moving a demurrer has not the right to open and conclude upon that demurrer. He is the promovent—he moves the demurrer—he opens the argument; counsel for respondent replies; counsel for demurrer concludes the argument. When we take into consideration the rules of practice of the State of Georgia, this view must be admitted to be perfectly correct. These rules are too well settled by this Court, and all other Courts, to need argument here.

The explanation of the Judge in regard to this matter does not seem to me to throw much light on it; but even admitting his explanation to be correct, how does that help? *We* moved the demurrer; we filed it; and we were entitled to the advantage of the conclusion, if any advantage were in it. Yet we were overruled.

What does the Judge say on this subject?

"The defendant then presented said demurrer, or exception, filed by him, copy of which is hereto annexed, marked (B), and insisted he had the right to open and conclude the argument on the demurrer. The Court, upon consideration, ruled that the plaintiff had the right to open and conclude said argument, and so allowed said plaintiff; and thereupon the defendant then and now excepts and assigns said ruling for error."

That was all that was put into the original bill of exceptions. The Judge interpolates the bill of exceptions with this: "The counsel for the defendant had already put in a demurrer to the application for *quo warranto* and withdrawn it. He had filed an answer and prayed an issue. He had moved a continuance upon the issue made by his answer, which continuance was refused," all of which we had a right to do without prejudicing the demurrer. We had a perfect right to put in an answer raising an issue of fact, and to move a continuance upon that answer; and, as stated before, without prejudicing our rights upon the demurrer. Defendant's counsel then called up his demurrer, after the continuance had been refused, "which," the Judge says, "would properly have been heard after the verdict upon the issue." After the case had been tried, and the verdict of the Jury rendered, then we might have the benefit of the argument on the demurrer! The reason why we could not have the conclusion, it is stated, was because the defendant called up his demurrer, "which would properly have been heard after the verdict upon the issue, as the answer suspended, if it did not overrule the demurrer!" That is the first time I have ever heard of a demurrer being "suspended," if it was not "overruled!" The case to be first heard and tried, and the verdict of the jury rendered, and then we should have a right to argue the demurrer!

"The counsel for the Relator—whilst not objecting to the argument of the legal point at the time—insisted that as the demurrer had been originally withdrawn and an answer had been filed, and the argument asked for by counsel for the defendant was to settle all the legal questions in the case, that the Relator, as the *promovent* in the case, was entitled to the conclusion of the argument." In that I contend that the Judge erred. On page 10 of the papers in this case [page 18 of this Book] he says that the demurrer had been withdrawn, but his explanations here show that it had not been withdrawn. The petition we did demur to, on the 26th of January, and that demurrer was withdrawn; the information was issued, and we then filed our demurrer, and filed an answer. The demurrer filed on the 4th of March, at the same time with the filing of the answer, *never was withdrawn.*

JUDGE McCAY. Is that demurrer a part of the record?

COL. STONE. Yes, sir; both demurrers are part of the record. You will find the demurrer to which he alludes, but which never was withdrawn, on page 5 of the record, [page 8 of this book.] That is the demurrer that was put in with the answer; but the demurrer to the *application* you will find on page 16 of the Record, [page 25 of this book.] The demurrer and answer filed on the 4th of March are the demurrer and answer that were filed to the *information*—not the demurrer filed to the petition; that had been withdrawn. Counsel on the other side will not argue that fact, I think.

COL. HARTRIDGE. I think we will.

COL. STONE. Very well, sir; I think it clearly proven by the record itself. I was not present at the time, but such I understand to be the explanation given by the learned Judge in the Bill of Exceptions—the reason being, he says, that "the counsel for the defendant had already put in a demurrer to the application for a *quo warranto*, and withdrawn it," while the fact is that the memorandum attached here to the demurrer which had not been withdrawn, and which is dated 4th of March, should have been attached by the Judge to the demurrer which was first filed to the application for the writ.

Further on, the Bill of Exceptions states:

"The argument on the demurrer having been concluded, the Court overruled the demurrer, deciding that under the Constitution and laws of Georgia a person of color was ineligible to office. To which decision of the Court overruling the demurrer, the defendant then and now excepts and assigns the same for error."

That, may it please the Court, brings us to the main question of the case; and although it is next in order, in my brief, I desire first to present the other grounds of error.

I shall refer now to the testimony in the case. The testimony of Albert Jackson has reference to his acts as Register; and to so much as relates to the defendant being a man of color, the defendant objected. I will read it:

Albert Jackson sworn, and says: "I was one of the Registers in the year 1867. There was a check put after White's name to designate him as a colored man. A list designating persons which had been arranged by the Board was posted up at the Court House. I do not know whether or not it was there all the time during the election. From these facts, and seeing him several times in the company of colored persons, I took him to be one. I have seen Spaniards and Italians as dark as White. I believe White is reputed a person of color. That the list of the registered voters was put up in the Court House for two or three weeks before the election. That against the name of the defendant the letter C. was marked, indicating colored. The Registers left the list open for correction for three weeks before the election, and that White did not ask any correction."

There is no proof that White ever saw the register, or knew that the letters "p. c." or "c." had been put opposite his name. It is testimony that cannot affect him, and was calculated to mislead the jury. It is irrelevant and immaterial—"res inter alios acta."

The next objection is found in the testimony of Dr. Yonge. The Court overruled that objection also. The doctor says:

3

"I have been a practicing physician for twenty years; examined the respondent, and gave a certificate to the Knickerbocker Insurance Company as a mulatto. I have studied the science of Ethnology, but not a great deal; this study leads one to inquire the difference of races. I came to the conclusion, however, that respondent was a mulatto from external indications. I think any intelligent person could tell as well as I could, (if much among the negroes,) the difference between a white man and a person of color, from observation."

The defendant also objected to the testimony of J. S. Howard. He states that—

"This book in Court contains copies of all applications for life insurance to the Knickerbocker Life Insurance Company. The originals are all sent on to New York. This application, which is signed with the name of respondent, I think was signed by himself for his wife. I do not know his hand-writing; don't know whether he or his wife signed the name."

In this case, as in the others, the Court overruled the objection.

They offered this copy of a record of an Insurance Company. It was proven to be a copy of an original document which had been sent to New York. They did not prove any diligence towards procuring the original, nor did they prove the loss of that original. They introduced this *secondary* evidence without proving any necessity therefor. In any view that may be taken of the law, I think that the admission of this copy, without accounting for the original record, was wrong—was error in the Court.

I desire here to call the attention of the Court briefly to the charge of the Court below. The Bill of Exceptions of the plaintiff in error states that—

"The plaintiff here closed. The defendant offered no testimony, and after argument had, the defendant requested the Court to charge the jury that the defendant, being in the exercise of the functions of the office, the presumption of the law is that he is entitled to it; and it is incumbent on the plaintiff to rebut such presumption by legal proof, and if plaintiff should fail to make out every point in his case, they must find for the defendant; which charge the Court refused to give."

I merely call the attention of the Court to that point, and will allow my associate counsel to argue it, as it was he who argued it in the Court below.

The main question of this case, may it please the Court, is this: Whether, under the Constitution and laws of Georgia, a person of color is ineligible to office?

Eligibility, in its legal sense, I understand to mean "qualified to be chosen—the legal right to be elected." And my first proposition is, that under the amended Constitution of the United States and the Constitution and laws of the State of Georgia, all citizens of this State, without regard to race or color—subject only to certain express restrictions named in the Constitution and laws of Georgia—are eligible to hold office.

Mr. Bouvier, in defining the word "citizen," says: "In American law: one who, under the Constitution and laws of the United States has a right to vote for representatives in Congress, and other public officers, and who is qualified to fill offices in the gift of the people."

I will admit, may it please the Court, that anterior to the adoption of the Constitutional amendment, the Constitution and laws were understood to refer only to white citizens; and it was presumed that only white persons were citizens: but since the adoption of the amendment the word citizens includes all persons born or naturalized in the United States.

I will first read, your Honors, the Constitutional amendment known as the 14th article:

"All persons born or naturalized in the United States, and subject to the jurisdiction thereof, are citizens of the United States, and of the State wherein they reside. No State shall make or inforce any law which shall abridge the privileges or immunities of citizens of the United States; nor shall any State deprive any person of life, liberty or property without due process of law; nor deny to any person within its jurisdiction the equal protection of its laws."

I will now read the second section of the first article of the Constitution of the State of Georgia:

"All persons born or naturalized in the United States and resident in this State, are hereby declared citizens of this State, and no law shall be made or enforced which shall abridge the privileges or immunities of citizens of the United States or of this State, or deny to any person within its jurisdiction the equal protection of its laws; and it shall be the duty of the General Assembly, by appropriate legislation, to protect every person in the due enjoyment of the rights, privileges and immunities guaranteed in this Constution."

The language—as said by Judge Schley—of these two sections, the first section of the 14th Constitutional amendment, and the second section of article first of the Constitution of Georgia, is almost identical. The third section of the 14th amendment goes on to recite some exceptions, as that " no person shall be a Senator or Representative in Congress, or elector of President and Vice President, or hold any office, civil or military, under the United States or under any State, who, having previously taken an oath as a member of Congress, or as an officer of the United States, or as a member of any State Legislature, or as an Executive or Judicial officer of any State, to support the Constitution of the United States, shall have engaged in insurrection or rebellion against the same, or given aid or comfort to the enemies thereof; but Congress may, by a vote of two-thirds of each House, remove such disability." That is the only disability mentioned in the 14th amendment to the Constitution of the United States. Certain persons are by that amendment made ineligible to certain offices, but *color* is not one of the features of ineligibility. I will also read sections 1 and 2, article 2 of the Constitution of this State:

"SECTION I. In all elections, by the People, the Electors shall vote by ballot.

"SECTION II. Every male person, born in the United States, and every male person who has been naturalized, or who has legally declared his intention to become a citizen of the United States, twenty-one years old, or upward, who shall have resided in this State six months next preceding the election, and shall have resided thirty days in the county in which he offers to vote, and shall have paid all taxes which may have been required of him, and which he may have had an opportunity of paying, agreeably to law, for the year next preceding the election, (except as hereinafter provided) shall be deemed an Elector : and every male citizen of the United States, of the age aforesaid, (except as hereinafter provided) who may be a resident of the State at the time of the adoption of this Constitution, shall be deemed an Elector, and shall have all the rights of an Elector, as aforesaid.   *   *   * "

I am clearly of opinion that this last provision refers to

all citizens. That negroes are citizens no one will dispute. They were made so by the 14th amendment to the Constitution of the United States, and by the Constitution of the State of Georgia.

Judge Schley's argument is that citizenship in its broadest sense includes everybody—men, women and children ; and that if we contend that citizenship carries with it the right to vote and hold office, it grants these privileges also to women and children. But speaking of "Electors," this second section, which I have just quoted, says that they shall be composed of "every *male* person born in the United States, and every *male* person who has been naturalized, or who has legally declared his intention, &c." A negro man is certainly a " male person." The plaintiff in error was "born in the United States." He is therefore an "Elector." The right of all qualified electors to hold office, is expressly conferred by the Code, as I shall now show.

By turning to section 1648 of the Code, it will be observed that " among the rights of *citizens* are the enjoyment of personal security, personal liberty, private property, and the disposition thereof, the elective franchise "—what else ? "*the right to hold office*, to testify as a witness, to perform any *civil function*, and to keep and bear arms."

It seems to me that if the sovereign people of the State, in convention assembled, have declared the negro to be a citizen, and the Code of this State declares that " among the rights of citizens shall be * * the right to hold office * * "—the conclusion is inevitable that the plaintiff in error is entitled to hold office and to exercise the functions of Clerk of the Superior Court. The next section of the Code makes our case the stronger, for it says that "*All citizens are entitled to exercise all their rights as such, unless specially prohibited by law.*" (Sec. 1649.)

Now, let us see if he has been "prohibited" from holding office. What class of persons are excluded from the right to hold office, in Georgia? Sections 3, 4 and 5, of Article two, of our State Constitution, say :

"Sec. III. No person convicted of felony or larceny before any court of this State, or of, or in the United States, shall be eligible to any office or appintment of honor or trust within this State, unless he shall have been pardoned.

"Sec. IV. No person who is the holder of any public mo-

neys shall be eligible to any office in this State, until the
same is accounted for and paid into the Treasury.

"Sec. V. No person who, after the adoption of this Constitution, being a resident of this State, shall engage in a
duel in this State, or elsewhere, or shall send or accept a
challenge, or be aider or abettor to such duel, shall vote or
hold office in this State; and every such person shall also
be subject to such punishment as the law may prescribe."

And section 6, of the same article, says:

"The General Assembly may provide, from time to time,
for the registration of all electors; but the following classes
of persons shall not be permitted to register, vote, or hold
office: First. Those who shall have been convicted of treason, embezzlement of public funds, malfeasance in office,
crime punishable by law with imprisonment in the Penitentiary, or bribery. Second. Idiots or insane persons."

A negro is not embraced in either of these sections, unless he comes specially under one or the other of the enumerated offenses. If the convention which framed this Constitution desired to exclude the negro, as such, from holding
office, why did they not, when making these exceptions, declare that although a colored man was a citizen, he should
not hold office? Clearly, the Constitution never had any
such design. They thought, as everybody thought, and as
the law distinctly laid down, that "citizens" having the
right to hold office, and the negro being a "citizen," it necessarily and incontrovertibly followed that he had the right
to hold office.
Let us glance at that ordinance of our Constitutional
Convention which defined the conditions for eligibility to
membership of the General Assembly at its first session. It
reads as follows:

"*Be it ordained by the people of Georgia, in Convention
assembled,* That the persons eligible as members of the General Assembly at the first election held under the Constitution framed by this Convention, shall be *citizens of the
United States who shall have been inhabitants of this State
for six months,* and of the District or County for which they
shall be elected for three months next preceding such election, and who, in the case of Senators, shall have attained
the age of twenty-five years, and in the case of Representatives, the age of twenty-one years, at the time of such elec-
t ."

The Constitution, article 4, section 3, says:

"No person shall be eligible to the office of Governor who shall not have been a citizen of the United States fifteen years and a citizen of this State six years, and who shall not have attained the age of thirty years."

Section 1050 of the Code says: "Females are not entitled to the privilege of the elective franchise, nor can they hold any civil office * * ." Section 120 paragraph one of the Code says that "all holders and receivers of public money of this State, or any county thereof, who have refused when called upon, or failed after reasonable opportunity to account for and pay over the same to the proper officers," shall be deemed ineligible to office. So, also, according to paragraph 3 of the same section, is "any person convicted or sentenced finally for any felony under the laws of this or any other State, involving moral turpitude, the offense being also a felony in this, unless restored by pardon from the proper Executive, under the great seal of the State, to all the rights of citizenship." Paragraph 6 says: "Persons of unsound mind, and those who from advanced age or bodily infirmity are unable to discharge the duties of the office to which they are chosen or appointed," shall also be deemed ineligible to office. These are not *all* the prohibitions that may be found, but they are nearly all; and in none of them, and in none of those that I have not read, is any distinction made as to *color*, nor any disqualification based on it.

I admit that a person may be a citizen in one sense, without having the right to vote—to exercise the elective franchise; but all persons allowed to exercise the elective franchise *must be* citizens. If they participate in the government they are citizens. The naturalization of an alien is a grant of citizenship, and carries with it the right to hold office. The enfranchisement of the *negro* is a grant of citizenship and carries with it the same right to hold office. It must have been considered by the makers of our Constitution that the process of naturalization carries with it the right to hold office. Hence they specially declared that a naturalized citizen could not be President of the United States, nor a Senator until after the lapse of nine years, nor a Representative until after the lapse of seven years, after his naturalization. If naturalization, therefore, did not carry with it the right to hold office, why this special Constitutional prohibition? I have seen no statute distinctly authorizing a naturalized citizen to hold office—*conferring* upon him that right. He was, before naturalization, a *foreigner* to all intents and purposes. When made a citizen of the United States he is a citizen for all purposes. Hence we see naturalized foreigners in the Congress of the United States, and filling various important offices of trust, as well in this State as elsewhere. And yet there is no law declaring that a naturalized citizen may hold office. Why? Because when he is made a citizen he- *acquires* the right to hold office, independent of any statutory provision on the subject.

It seems to me too clear for dispute that the Congress that framed and adopted the 14th amendment to the Federal Constitution, and the Convention which framed the present Constitution of Georgia, intended the word "citizen," and the words "privileges and immunities of citizens," to be interpreted in their broadest and most comprehensive political sense, granting to the native born colored man all the rights, privileges and immunities belonging to the native born white man, or naturalized foreigner, not only the right to vote, but to hold office.

It should be borne in mind, too, that at the time this Constitutional Convention assembled, the people of the State of Georgia were legislating more particularly, perhaps, for the colored man than for any other class of the people of the State. There was greater necessity for it. For, as under the old law, in the language of Chief Justice Taney, that class of persons "had no rights which a white man was bound to respect," the intention clearly was to give them ample rights—as ample as any naturalized foreigner in this State had.

It was argued in the Court below that if the Constitutional Convention had intended to confer the right to hold office on persons of color, they would have done it in express terms, and not have left it to be inferred as an incident of citizenship. Not having done so, and having rejected what was then known as the 10th section of article 2 on Franchise and Elections, the conclusion is drawn that the Convention did not intend to confer the right to hold office on persons of color. It was in no wise necessary to place in the Constitution any such express provision. Article 11, section 3, of the new Constitution adopts, in subordination only to the Constitution of the United States and that of Georgia, the Code of laws known as "Irwin's Code." That Code, as I have shown, confers upon the *citizen*, by express provision, *the right to hold office*. Here, then, is an express grant, of the right to hold office, in the Code, and the Code is recognized as the law of the land by an express constitutional provision. The Constitution made the colored man a *citizen* and an elector, and if anything more was necessary to entitle him to hold office, the adoption of the Code fixed *that*. It would have been a work of supererogation to reaffirm what already was enacted and made certain by a positive provision of the Code. Therefore, there was no necessity for the said 10th section which was so often referred to by the Judge below in rendering his decision.

I shall not comment much on the argument of Judge Schley, but will leave that to my associate counsel, if he chooses to do so. I will quote one remark, however, from the learned Judge's decision. He says: "If the Convention had given in express terms the right to hold office, the silence as to the elective franchise would be proper, not to say logical, because the right to hold office necessarily carries with it the right to vote. I can put no other construction on this action of the convention than that they meant to give only such rights as are given in express terms ;" and he says further, "this conclusion is made certain by the record of their proceedings, which shows that they, by solemn vote, rejected the amendment which was offered to give the right to hold office to persons of color." Now, may it please the Court, I will read that "amendment" to which the Judge refers; and you will see that the word "color" never once occurs in it :

"Sec. 10. All qualified electors, and none others, shall be eligible to any office in this State, unless disqualified by the Constitution of this State, or by the Constitution of the United States."

I should like Judge Schley, or some other learned Judge, to show me where the Convention rejected any "amendment" or anything else "which was offered to give the right to hold office to persons of color," as such.

I did not have the honor to be a member of the Convention, but in looking through the history of that body, the subsequent action that was taken on that section convinces me that there is some little unwritten history connected with that celebrated 10th section, and by referring to the old Constitution of the State, it may, perhaps, throw some light on the matter, at least inferentially. At the time that section was adopted, the Constitution was in embryo; it had not been adopted as a whole. The committees were at work adopting certain sections, and there were certain members who had, perhaps, some ambition to become members of the General Assembly. So I should judge, at least, from some of the names attached to that section when reported from the committee, and from the subsequent votes taken upon the section.

By the Constitution of Georgia, adopted on the 7th of November, 1865, it will be seen that six months' residence in the county and two years' in the State, were among the qualifications for an elector. And by the same Constitution a three years' residence in the State and one year in the county were among the necessary qualifications for a Senator or Representative. I submit whether the inference is not strong if not *conclusive* that the said tenth section did not refer to colored men at all, but was moved to remove certain disabilities that were hanging over the heads of some of the members of that Convention, who were ambitious to become members of the General Assembly. They were qualified as electors and desired to remove any doubt that might arise as to their eligibility to office. I may be wrong in my surmises, but that is the view I take of it, and this view is supported by the subsequent action of the Convention. For Mr. Martin, (of Habersham,) offered, on the 13th of February, 1868, as a substitute for the 10th section, the following:

"No person who is a disqualified elector, or who is disfranchised by the Constitution of Georgia, shall be eligible to any office in this State."

This however, was not adopted.

Then Mr. Crane, (of Towns,) proposed to amend said section by inserting after the word "electors," in the first line thereof the words, "who have been citizens of the United States for seven years." That, on being put to a vote, was rejected—yeas 33, nays 89. Here then, was a good opportunity to have fixed the status of the colored man, and to render him ineligible to office for seven years. It provided in express terms for such a result; and yet it was defeated by a majority of 56. And when the Convention came to a vote on the 10th section, the motion to strike it out was carred by a majority of 114.

I ask then, how it can be said that "the Convention rejected, by a solemn vote, the amendment intending to conter, by express terms, the right to hold office, upon the colored man." No class is mentioned. The whole action of the Convention refutes the assertion. Colored men, among others, voted to strike out; and who can suppose that they would vote to disfranchise themselves?

An officer, may it please the Court, is but the *servant of the people.* He has to do their will. By no reasonable argument can it be shown that the Constitutional Convention intended to disfranchise ninety thousand legal voters in the State of Georgia, that is to say, render them ineligible to office. The last registration which we have of this State shows, I believe, about 100,000 white voters, and some 90,000 black. Are these latter ninety thousand, who are liable to taxation, road duty, milita duty, &c., to be excluded from official position if their friends of their own color and kindred choose to vote for and elect them? In that case you would soon hear a revival of the cry of "taxation without representation." Open the doors to all; the ignorant will not get office often, if they get it at all. Let all men have an opportunity of at least showing what they can do for themselves. Do not tell a man that he must go to the polls and vote at another man's bidding. Let him vote for whomsoever he chooses; and if the candidate for whom he votes is of his own kin or color, who shall blame him? Let not the color of the skin, nor the character of the hair be the guide of action. Rather let competence and worth, intelligence and ability, be the standard—a standard that will work well alike for all.

What I have intended to show in the preceding argument is—

First. That the Constitution of the State makes colored persons citizens.

Second. That it adopts the Code, known as Irwin's Code of Georgia, as embracing the Statutes of force in Georgia.

Third. The Code provides that among the rights of citizens is the Elective Franchise and the right to hold office.

Fourth. That all the citizens of Georgia are entitled to exercise all their rights as such, unless specially prohibited by law.

Fifth. That colored citizens are not excepted, much less "specially prohibited by law," from holding office in Georgia.

If I have established those propositions, it follows that the Respondent in the Court below is entitled to hold his office as Clerk of the Superior Court of the County of Chatham, and that the Court erred in overruling the Demurrer.

ARGUMENT OF COL. HARTRIDGE.

Col. Julian Hartridge, opening for the Defendant in Error, said :

MAY IT PLEASE THE COURT :

There are certain preliminary, or outside, questions involved in this case, to which it is necessary that I should first call your Honors' attention. When I say *outside* questions, I mean outside the *great* questions or points involved in this case—the verdict of the jury and the decision of the Court below.

I shall make no comments on the course of the Judge below, in requesting or requiring—whichever it might have been—the counsel for the Plaintiff in Error to incorporate his Decision in the Bill of Exceptions, or the record : that is a matter which cannot affect the decision in this case one way or the other; but the Plaintiff in Error complains of the Court below, in the first place, because he refused to grant the motion for the continuance asked for, and referred to in the Bill of Exceptions.

That motion, may it please the Court, occurred in this way. Upon the filing of a Demurrer by the Plaintiff in Error, to the original Application for leave to file a *Quo Warranto*, a continuance was moved upon the ground of the absence of Counsel, which motion the Court overruled because leading counsel was present. That Demurrer was then withdrawn, and an issue of fact was filed. Upon the filing of the issue of fact the continuance was granted, and the case was put down for trial on the 22d day of March.

I may as well say here that we are to go by the record in this case, and nothing else. I am not disposed—and if I were disposed this Court would not permit me—to enter into a controversy with the counsel for the Plaintiff in Error as to what were the precise facts in the Court below. This Court must go by the Record. Upon that alone, therefore, I shall predicate my argument.

Upon the 22d day of March, at the time when the case was assigned for trial, and for which time the jury had been drawn, under a special Act of the Legislature of Georgia in contemplation of the trial of cases of *quo warranto*—at that time the counsel then reported. The Plaintiff in Error moved for a continuance on the ground that his commissions had not been returned; that the testimony which he expected to elicit by the witnesses to be examined by commission, was material—setting forth the facts. But, in that affidavit, it was nowhere sworn or stated that the affidavit or motion was made—not for the purpose of delay—but for the purpose of being able to obtain this testimony, nor was it stated in that affidavit or motion for a continuance that there was no other witness present by whom he, the party, could prove the facts as in the other case. The Court refused on these two grounds; and I respectfully submit that the Court was right.

Counsel for the Plaintiff in Error say that the Court was wrong, because of an express statute which declares that whenever a motion is made for the continuance of a cause, in consequence of the non-return of a commission which has been sued out, it shall be governed by the same rules as the affidavit in reference to the materiality of testimony in the case of an absent witness—where a party moves for a continuance on account of the absence of a living witness. Now, he contends that the fact of the statute simply mentioning that the affidavit shall contain a statement in reference to the materiality of the testimony, excludes the necessity for any other statement to be made in that affidavit. To what a consequence would such a conclusion bring this Court? If his position be correct, a party who moves a continuance in his case because his commission has not been returned, has only to swear that the testimony is material, and set forth the facts, and that is all! Term after term that testimony may fail to come. At the very first term the affidavit may be made for the purpose of delaying over. There may be truth in the fact alleged, that there *is* such a witness, whether in Alaska, San Francisco, or elsewhere. There may be no truth in a witness living within the strict borders of the United States—or the strict limit allowed. There may be no truth that that witness could prove the facts alleged. It may be true that an affidavit is made sometimes for delay. It may be true that there are other witnesses present who can prove the same facts; and yet upon such an affidavit, containing this single, solitary, isolated fact, unsupported by any evidence that it is being sought in good faith, the Court is *compelled* by the position taken by counsel to grant the continuance. I respectfully submit that such is not law, and that such has been declared to be not law by the Supreme Court of Georgia.

It was the rule upon which continuances were granted, before the adoption of this Code, that the applications were controlled or governed by the requisitions, or rather the requirements of the rules of Court. There was no statute upon the subject, but the rule of Court became a statute by virtue of the law which authorized the adoption of these rules of Court.

Now, these rules of Court bearing upon the absence of living witnesses, declare that certain things shall be stated in these affidavits; but it was no where said that the party should be compelled to swear that he had no witnesses present by whom he intended to prove the facts specially to be proven by the absent witness. It was then not a portion of the statute of the State, any more than it is now a portion of the statute, in reference to witnesses to be examined under commission. And yet the Supreme Court of Georgia, in just such a case, made the following decision. I read from 10th Georgia Reports, page 19:

"But to the affidavit. An affidavit for a continuance should be full, satisfactory, and direct as to the material allegations necessary for a continuance." There are material allegations necessary for a continuance, outside of any rule of Court—outside of any statute. The rule of Court says certain things must be sworn to; the statute says certain other things must be sworn to, but they no where state that it is not necessary that other things should be sworn to. No Court is bound to grant a continuance unless it is convinced that it is asked for in good faith, and *absolutely necessary* for the attainment of justice upon the part of the applicant. If the Court sees that it is not done in good faith—if the party is not willing to swear that he does not make his affidavit for delay only, or is not willing to swear that he has no other witness by whom he can prove the same facts, the Court is not bound to continue. "This affidavit," says the Court, in the case just alluded to, "does not state whether in fact there be any other witnesses except Hardy Bryan, nor that the matter expected to be proved by him, could not be established by any other witness present." There the Supreme Court of Georgia declared that the requirements in an application for a continuance are beyond the rule of Court, and beyond the statute referred to by counsel. The Court must be convinced that the party is powerless unless this be granted. Therefore I submit that the Court below did right in refusing to continue.

The next point, may it please the Court, is that the Court below erred in reference to allowing the opening and con-

clusion to the parties in opposition. I shall predicate my
position on the facts; I shall enter into no discussion or controversy, but take the record as it stands, upon the statement
made by the Court below.

The Respondent below—the plaintiff in error here—filed
on the 4th of March a demurrer, as he called it, in writing,
and an issuable plea as to facts. Now, just there the
learned counsel is mistaken—with all due deference to him—
when he says that the law of Georgia, in common law cases,
allows pleas and demurrers, &c., to be filed at the same time.
I understand no such thing in the common law of Georgia,
as written demurrers. except in criminal cases.

The defendant had, however, filed a written demurrer;
that is he had stated in writing that, admitting the facts,
they did not show such a state of circumstances as would
warrant the legal interpretation sought by the Relator's *quo
warranto.* But the Judge tells you that this demurrer,
dated 4th of March and filed on the same day, as was also
the answer—the issuable fact which was raised,—" The foregoing demurrer was withdrawn on the day it was filed." In
other words, the right to take oral exceptions, when he had
no other right, was withdrawn. The application for oral
exceptions was withdrawn on the same day that notice was
given. The issue of fact was left alone. What was that
issue? That this man was not a negro. Upon that issue
the case was to go to the jury. The jury had been summoned
on the 4th of March, and empaneled on the 22d. On that
day, when moved to go to trial, the counsel for the respondent—the plaintiff in error—first asked the Court to hear
his exceptions—exceptions which were the same as the written demurrer, " which was withdrawn." says the Judge.
What further says the Court? "Counsel for Relator made no
objection to have it at that time." We were willing to take
the question then, or during the course of the trial. We had
no objection to hearing it then. It was simply a question
of hearing then, the exceptions in law which could be heard
in the course of the trial. He was ruled to trial, and the
Court in effect said, "I will hear your legal argument now,
with the consent of counsel for the other side; but that is
all," and the Court decided that we could open and conclude. But suppose the Court erred in concluding that
counsel for the Relator had the right to open and conclude,
will this Court, provided the decision of the Court below be
correct send this case back to be argued over again in a different order? If the Judge below has arrived at a correct conclusion on the great question involved in the case, will you

say to him, "You are right in your decision, but we want
you to have it argued over again in another form of argument." The whole question, therefore, amounts to this: Is
the Court correct in its decision? If so it would be waste
of time for this Court to send it back to him and tell him
that his *decision* is correct, but that the case must be gone
through with again. I will refer you to two cases, to show
you that I am right in this. One case will be found in the
4th Georgia Reports, 360, "Where there has been no violation of any rule of law, and the facts of the case have been
fairly submitted to the jury by the Court, a new trial will
not be granted." "We have," says the Court, "carefully
examined the other grounds of error taken for a new trial,
as certified by the presiding Judge, together with his charge
to the jury, as contained in the record before us, and the
evidence; all of which, to our minds, do not furnish any
legal ground for a new trial. The law of the case, as well
as the facts, appears to have been fairly submitted to the
jury by the Court below, and the judgment of the Court below is therefore affirmed."

Now, if the law in this case, upon the question of Demurrer, as it stood, was fairly submitted to the Court, and fairly
decided by the Court, why send it back simply because the
sequence or order of the argument was not correct?

In the 6th Georgia Reports I find a decision of the same
Court to the same effect: "When the Court below fairly
submits the facts of a case to the consideration of the jury,
and there is no error in law, the Court will not disturb the
verdict of that jury." There is, therefore, to my mind no
reason why, if this Court holds the decision of the Court
below to be correct, your Honors should disturb that decision merely because of an error in the order of the argument.

The next error assigned by the respondent is as to the
admission of the testimony of Jackson, relating to his acts
as Register, and the reputation of White as to his being a
person of color. That testimony is as follows:

"I was one of the Registers in the year 1867. There was
a check put after White's name to designate him as a colored man. A list designating persons, which had been
arranged by the Board, was posted up at the Court House.
I do not know whether or not it was there all the time
during the election. From these facts, and seeing him several times in company with colored persons, I took him to

be one. I have seen Spaniards and Italians as dark as White. I believe White is reputed a person of color. That the list of the registered voters was put up in the Court House for two or three weeks before the election. That against the name of the Defendant the letter C was marked, indicating colored. The Registers left the list open for correction for three weeks before the election, and that White did not ask any correction."

It is maintained that the status of a person as a slave, or a free person of color, cannot be proved by reputation. I submit that the Supreme Court of Georgia has decided otherwise in a case found in 20th Georgia, 480. This was the case in which a question was involved whether a certain party was a free person of color or not. At page 508 will be found the following: "Was it competent for the witnesses, Joseph Bush and Mary Rogers, to testify as to the general reputation, in the neighborhood where he resided, that Joseph Nunez was a free person of color, and that such was their own belief? Mr. Greenleaf says: 'Upon the same principle it is considered that evidence of general reputation, reputed ownership, public rumor, general notoriety, and the like, though composed of the speech of third persons, not under oath, is original evidence, and not hearsay, the subject of inquiry being of many voices to the same fact.' (1 Greenleaf Ev. § 101.) As to the opinion of the witnesses, it was given in connection with, and as a mental deduction from, all the facts which come within their knowledge, and to which they had deposed."

Now, in this case the witness testifies as to the general reputation of this party as a person of color. He testifies as to the facts on which he based his opinion. The authority says these are competent. It is for the jury to say whether the facts are properly submitted. All the declarations in the testimony of Jackson as to his acts as Register went for the same purpose. They went to show the reputation—the opinion formed of this man White—whether or not he was a person of color. Jackson gives no secondary testimony, or testimony of what other people did. He gives testimony as to acts of which he was *particeps*. He says that he, with other registers, put the letter "c" opposite this man's name, and that he formed the opinion that he was colored from seeing him with colored people. That letter "c" was put there so that those might object who wanted to do so. He did not apply to correct it, although he was an applicant for office. Whether he saw it or not is not material.

The next error 1 find is as to the testimony of Dr. Yonge, founded on his medical knowledge and his opinion based on that knowledge, in his examination of White. Dr. Yonge testifies as follows:

"I have been a practicing physician for twenty years; examined the Respondent, and gave a certificate to the Knickerbocker Insurance Company as a mulatto. I have studied the science of Ethnology, but not a great deal; this study leads one to enquire the difference of races. I came to the conclusion, however, that Respondent was a mulatto from external indications. I think any intelligent person could tell as well as I could, (if much among the negroes,) the difference between a white man and a person of color, from observation."

It makes no difference whether a layman may be able to do the same thing as a physician or not. A physician is an expert in the eyes of the law.

Dr. J. S. Howard, sworn, says: "This book in Court contains all applications for life insurance to the Knickerbocker Life Insurance Company. The originals are all sent on to New York. This application, which is signed with the name of Respondent, I think was signed by himself for his wife. I do not know his hand-writing; don't know whether he or his wife signed the name."

Now, it was objected that this was secondary testimony. Secondary testimony is good testimony in some cases. The law does not always require *original* testimony; if it did, it would sometimes defeat its own object—justice. I need not cite to this Court in proof of this position. I hold that where the primary testimony is beyond the jurisdiction of the Court, secondary testimony can be admitted: and why? Because the Court cannot force before it the *original*. If it has no power to compel the production of *original* testimony, secondary testimony is good. If the Court had no power to compel the attendance of a witness, his testimony by commission is good.

JUDGE McCAY: Does this paper purport to be signed by White, or by White's wife?

Col. Hartridge: It is signed "R. W. White, for his wife;" that is the rule of the insurance company; it is an insurance on his life, in favor of his wife.

Governor Johnson, (of Counsel for Plaintiff in Error): I will take the liberty of interrupting you to say that if the original were there, it would not be evidence: there is no proof that he ever signed it.

Col. Hartridge: Very well, sir. The copy was admitted in this case because the original was beyond the jurisdiction of the Court. The 21st Georgia Reports, page 219, decides this general proposition: "If the primary evidence is not attainable, secondary is admissible." The 26th Georgia, page 544, says: "When a paper is beyond the jurisdiction of the Court, verbal evidence of its contents is admissible."

The counsel says he will contend that even if the original had been in Court, it could not be admitted, because there is no testimony to show that White had signed it. I will read again the testimony of Dr. Howard:

"This book in Court contains copies of all applications for life insurance to the Knickerbocker Life Insurance Company. The originals are all sent on to New York. This application, which is signed with the name of respondent, I think was signed by himself for his wife. I do not know his hand-writing; don't know whether he or his wife signed the name."

The original was required to be signed by him. That original had been sent to the Insurance Company at New York: this copy had been regularly made, was testified to as being a correct copy, and therefore the Court received it as the best secondary evidence of the fact, that could be obtained.

The learned counsel objects also to the charge of the Judge. What was that charge? It was not specifically and technically in the language asked for by the counsel, but did it not cover the law in the case? He says, "I am requested to charge you on the character of the testimony, that where blood, race, &c., is the subject that you can take general hearsay, or the reputation of the person in his community, that is, what he says of himself—what others say of him, his associates and his general reputation as such in the community in which he resides, &c., in order to determine as to his being a white man or a person of color."

And so says the Supreme Court of Georgia, in the case in 20th Georgia, to which I have already alluded. The Judge, in the case now before this Court, says further, " Under slavery no records were kept of births or marriages among slaves, and hence the rule as to general reputation and hearsay was more applicable to blacks than to whites. Now you must look to the testimony and be satisfied in your own minds that the facts disclose one-eighth or more of negro or African blood in the veins of the Respondent before you can find for the Relator." That was the fact in issue, and the Judge says: " You must look to the testimony and be satisfied in your own minds that the facts disclose one-eighth or more of negro or African blood in the veins of the Respondent, before you can find for the Relator."

Judge Schley continues : " I am further requested by the defendant to charge you ' that the defendant being in the discharge of the functions of the office, the presumption of the law is that he is entitled to the office, and it is incumbent in the plaintiff to rebut such presumption by legal proof, and if the plaintiff should fail to make out every point in his case, you must find for the defendant.' I cannot charge you in the language asked for, but I do charge you as a general principle of law, that any person holding an office the law presumes him eligible and competent to hold the same, but that presumption refers to his acts as such officer where the rights of others were affected, such as attestator and other acts in the line of his office."

According to the Code, an officer *de facto* is a good officer, and his acts as such are good, whether he be an officer *de jure* or not. But when the issue is made in a case in which he is a party himself, there is no such presumption ; or in the language of the Judge, " where, as in this case, the official had no reference to any official act, but as to the race or blood of the defendant disqualifying him from holding office, there was *not* such presumption of law as contemplated by the language contained in the request to charge."

Now, what was the point? That the Respondent had one-eighth or more of negro or African blood in his veins—the only issue of fact. The Court says, " You must be satisfied" of that before you can find for the Relator. While then this charge of the Judge may or may not happen to be in precisely the proper language, if it does not violate the law, it is correct.

There is no application made to this Court for a new trial upon the ground of a verdict contrary to the charge of the

Court. The verdict of the jury is not contrary to the charge, and the evidence is presumed to have been sufficient. Therefore, that cannot be entertained ; but the only question is, was the Judge correct in giving the principles of the law so as to protect the respondent in his rights, and was he right in ruling in the matter as he did ? If so, that settles the matter.

Having thus disposed of the preliminary questions, I now come to the main issue in this case. It is a question that has been so widely, and so ably, and so elaborately argued on different occasions in this State—a question that has been so much the object of universal public attention that it strikes me it needs but a very brief argument on our part. It is a question to which the mind of every reasoning or thinking man has been directed, and upon which some one opinion or another has always been made. I shall, therefore, content myself with giving a brief exposition of the arguments, &c., entering into no elaboration or detail—a duty which I shall leave to my associate counsel, should he deem it necessary to be done.

The great complaint, may it please the Court, is that the Honorable Judge of the Court below decided that a person of color, having one-eighth or more of negro blood in his veins, is not eligible to office in Georgia. He predicated that decision upon the Constitution of the United States, the Constitution of the State of Georgia, and the statute law of the State of Georgia. That is, he decided that neither the Constitution of the United States nor the Constitution of Georgia, nor the statute law of Georgia, having conferred this privilege upon him, he had no right to exercise it. Why did he make that decision?

May it please your Honor, in order to determine that matter it is necessary to go back for but a very few years to the former condition of this present applicant for the right to hold office, or rather to the condition of the race to which he belongs, as found by this jury below.

The negro population of Georgia had no rights under the law save the right of protection of the person under the criminal laws, equal with the white man. They did have that. It was the boast of the slavery institution that so far as the law was concerned, it gave the life of the slave the same protection beneath the ægis of the Constitution that it gave to the white man. The humblest slave that crawled upon the face of the State had, when he stood in the Court room, with life or limb imperilled, equal rights with the proudest freeman that claimed him as his slave. Those were all the rights he had. The right to his person, the right to his labor, the right to his services, and to the product of his labor—all belonged to the white man. He had no natural rights belonging to a freeman; that is, no natural rights in the State recognized by the decisions of the Supreme Court of the United States and other Courts, except this right of protection to person and life, given by the Constitution of the State itself.

But, in the change of events—by the result of war—put it, if you please, under the Emancipation proclamation, or under the Convention of Georgia—his chains fell from his limbs: that is, his imaginary chains. He became a freeman, and was elevated to the same standard as all freemen in all lands in the known world. That is, he became possessed of certain inalienable personal rights, by being emancipated. These rights were given to him by the Legislature of Georgia, in definite terms, by statute. They gave him the right to go into the courts, to sue and be sued; the right to testify in certain cases; the right to have his person and property protected; the right to pursue the path of knowledge, or of wealth—and the acquisition of the one or the other just like a white man. They gave him these inalienable personal rights: no man could thenceforward lay his hand upon him and say, "You are my slave." They gave him that, and nothing more.

Then came the Fourteenth Amendment—passed by the Congress of the United States—which made him a citizen of the United States. Then came the Constitution of the State of Georgia—that gave him the same rights, he being a "male person." These two gave him the inalienable natural rights of a citizen; but nothing else. They simply contemplated giving him the rights of a freeman, and taking away from the legislative power the right to take them away from him. They made him a citizen just as they made women citizens, and as they made infants citizens. They gave him the same inalienable rights that infants have—nothing more, nothing less. These were given him by the Fourteenth Amendment. There is no necessity to go back of that, to the Civil Rights Bill. They are all merged in the Fourteenth Amendment, which is copied, almost literally, in the Constitution of Georgia.

The Fourteenth Amendment to the Constitution says:

"Section 1. All persons born or naturalized in the United

States, and subject to the jurisdiction thereof, are citizens of the United States, and of the State wherein they reside. No State shall make or inforce any law which shall abridge the privileges or immunities of citizens of the United States; nor shall any State deprive any person of life, liberty or property without due process of law; nor deny to any person within its jurisdiction the equal protection of its laws."

The Constitution of Georgia, section 2, Article 1, says:

" All persons born or naturalized in the United States and resident in this State, are hereby declared citizens of this State, and no law shall be made or enforced which shall abridge the privileges or immunities of citizens of the United States or of this State, or deny to any person within its jurisdiction the equal protection of its laws; and it shall be the duty of the General Assembly, by appropriate legislation, to protect every person in the due enjoyment of the rights, privileges and immunities guaranteed in this section."

These clauses give him the rights, privileges and immunities of a citizen of the United States—nothing more, nothing less. What were the privileges and immunities of citizens of this State which they conferred upon him? They were these general, generic, natural rights inherent in all freemen.

I read from page 381, Washington's Circuit Court Reports, Vol. 4:

" The inquiry is, What are the privileges and immunities of citizens in the several States? We feel no hesitation in confining these expressions to those privileges and immunities which are, in their nature, fundamental; which belong, of right, to the citizens of all free governments; and which at all times have been enjoyed by the citizens of the several States which compose this Union from the time of their becoming free, independent and sovereign. What these fundamental principles are, it would perhaps be more tedious than difficult to enumerate. They may, however, be all comprehended under the following heads: protection by the government, the enjoyment of life and liberty, with the right to acquire and possess property of every kind, and to pursue and obtain happiness and safety; subject, nevertheless, to such restraints as the government may justly prescribe for the personal good of the whole. The right of a citizen of one State to pass through or to reside in any other State for purposes of trade, agriculture, professional pursuits, or otherwise; to claim the benefit of the writ of habeas corpus; to institute and maintain actions of any kind in the courts of the State; to take, hold and dispose of property, either real or personal; and an exemption from higher taxes or impositions than are paid by the other citizens of the State; may be mentioned as some of the particular privileges and immunities of citizens, which are clearly embraced by the general description of privileges deemed to be fundamental; to which may be added the elective franchise, as regulated and established by the laws or Constitution of the State in which it is to be exercised."

In the Dred Scott case, 19 Howard, the same thing is decided in the Supreme Court of the United States, from the lips of Chief Justice Taney:

"Undoubtedly," says he, "a person may be a citizen, that is, a member of the community who form the sovereignty, although he exercises no share of the political power, and is incapacitated from holding particular offices. Women and minors, who form a part of the political family, cannot vote; and when a property qualification is required to vote or hold a particular office, those who have not the necessary qualifications cannot vote or hold the office, yet they are citizens.

"So, too, a person may be entitled to vote by the law of the State who is not a citizen even of the State itself."

The Constitution of Georgia declares that only those are citizens who are either born or naturalized citizens of the United States, and yet the same Constitution gives the right to vote to a man who is not a citizen, but who has only declared his intention to become such.

"So, too," says Chief Justice Taney, in the decision just alluded to, "a person may be entitled to vote by the law of the State who is not a citizen even of the State itself. And in some of the States of the Union foreigners not naturalized are allowed to vote. And the State may give the right to free negroes and mulattoes, but that does not make them citizens of the State, and still less of the United States. And the provision in the Constitution giving privileges and immunities in other States does not apply to them.

"Neither does it apply to a person who, being the citizen of a State, migrates to another State. For then he becomes subject to the laws of the State in which he lives, and he is no longer a citizen of the State from which he removed. And the State in which he resides may then, unquestionably, determine his *status* or condition, and place him among the class of persons who are not recognized as citizens, but belong to an inferior and subject race; and may deny him the privileges and immunities enjoyed by its citizens.

"But so far as mere rights of person are concerned, the provision in question is confined to citizens of a State who are temporarily in another State without taking up their residence there. It gives them no political rights in the State as to voting or holding office, or in any other respect."

The learned Judge below referred to a case in 4 Dev., and a decision recently made by Justice Swayne, going to show that the fact of one's being invested with the rights of citizenship carries nothing with it but these inherent, *fundamental* rights common to a free people in all countries. The Constitution does not use the word "male" in connection with citizenship. It says "*All* persons born or naturalized," &c. The child that has breathed the breath of life but *one hour*, is a citizen as much as the man of eighty, who is trembling on the verge of the grave.

I take it, then, that the Fourteenth Amendment and the Constitution of the State of Georgia did not confer on a person of color the right to hold office. The Plaintiff in Error here was before deprived of all rights of a political character. He had but a portion of personal or fundamental rights. When, however, he was elevated to the position of a citizen, he was placed above the standard by which he had been formerly judged. He was given all these fundamental rights; and began to enjoy all the rights given to him by the Constitution and statutes of Georgia, and the Constitution of the United States; inalienable rights, which cannot now be taken from him except by sovereign act of the people, by a change in the Constitution of the United States. They did not carry with them the right to hold office, because, as the Court below says, the same right would have been carried to women, and even to children but just born.

Now, then, if the Constitution of the United States, by this general clause, and the Constitution of the State of Georgia, by this general clause, making them citizens of the United States, and of Georgia, did not give them the power to hold office, whence can the power be derived? It is said the Constitution of the State of Georgia did so, by another section, which declares that—

"Every male person born in the United States, and every male person who has been naturalized, or who has legally declared his intention to become a citizen of the United States, twenty-one years old or upward, who shall have resided in this State six months next preceding the election, and shall have resided thirty days in the county in which he offers to vote, and shall have paid all taxes which may have been required of him, and which he may have had an opportunity of paying agreeably to law, for the year next preceding the elction, (except as hereinafter provided) who may be a resident of the State at the time of the adoption of this Constitution, shall be deemed an elector, and shall have the rights of an elector as aforesaid."

Mark, now, that this clause of the Constitution confers the rights of an elector upon *a party who is not a citizen.* One clause declares that "All persons born in the United States or naturalized," &c., are *citizens ;* another—the one just quoted—gives to persons who are *not citizens* of Georgia *the right to vote.* A woman "born in the United States or naturalized," &c., cannot vote. A male infant, though he may be twenty years and eleven months old, with education, with intelligence, with appreciation of government and of polity, understanding the relations of governments and able to judge well the wise from the unwise, cannot even vote, though he is a citizen ; while those who are not citizens, but foreigners—subjects of another government, who at any time may abandon this country to return to their own government, and who in time of war may be claimed by that government—can vote in Georgia. The first right conferred—the fundamental right—is the right of protection, in property and in person, as the Supreme Court says. Upon that fundamental foundation, you build up a superstructure, and go up by degrees to the capstone. First, the fundamental rights ; then the right to vote—that is, the right to say who shall govern and control the country—who shall direct its legislation—who shall execute its laws. Then comes the right to be one of those who shall legislate—requiring the highest degree of intelligence—the very point of the pinnacle. That makes the privileges of the citizen full and complete; and enables the man possessing it to stand forth in his full proportions before the world as a full, free and competent citizen. First, protection in his rights. Second, investing him with the privilege of selecting who shall govern. Third, with that of governing himself.

The argument of the learned counsel that the right to vote

carries with it the right to be voted for, gives the right to be voted for to aliens, whose allegiance may be due to some other nation or sovereign, whose affections, whose memories, whose everything may lie beyond the ocean; while the intelligent and active young men and women of the State cannot do it.

It never was contemplated by this Constitution that the right to vote should carry with it the right to hold office. It is a principle of law that the construction of a statute is to be deduced from the language of the law itself and not from the individual declarations of legislators; when you want to judge of the intention of legislation, then the acts and sayings and doings of the body creating the law are pertinent to throw light on the subject.

The learned counsel refers to the 10th section—the section afterwards stricken out. It was proposed by a committee who must have been impressed with the necessity for such a provision, otherwise they would not have reported it. This section declared that all duly qualified electors and none others should be eligible to office. Now the article of the Constitution conferring suffrage had made the negro man an elector; therefore the declaration in that article to the effect that all electors would be competent to hold office included the black man. There was no necessity to mention his name. This section was stricken out by the Convention themselves. Why? We say because it was not intended to be there. The learned counsel contends that they didn't think it necessary to put it there, because they adopted the Code, and the Code declared that among the rights of citizens should be the right to hold office. But the Code had already declared the right to vote to be among the right of citizens, and yet it was thought necessary to put it in the Constitution. If it were unnecessary to put in the Constitution a section giving to colored people the right to hold office, it was equally unnecessary to put in a provision giving them the right to vote. We say the Constitution itself did not give the right to hold office. Without reading the authorities which the learned counsel will give who will follow me, I can refer you to the acts of the United States Congress. They conferred upon electors in the District of Columbia the right to vote, as will be shown by the statute which will be read to you. They conferred upon all citizens, irrespective of color, and all citizens in the territories, the right to vote, and yet they found it necessary afterwards to pass acts declaring that the black man had the power to hold office. The very discussion on the 15th amendment will speak for itself in this matter. When the Convention adopted the Constitution it is clear that they were not impressed with the idea that the right to vote carried with it the right to hold office. But it is said they knew the Code of Georgia conferred the right to hold office upon black men. Does the Code of Georgia confer that power? I have tried to show, your Honors, that the Constitution of the State of Georgia, in making them citizens, did not give them that right; nor did it give it to them by giving them the right to vote. Now, if the Constitution did not give it to them, does the statute law of the State do so? For, unless something gives it to them, they have it not. They had it not in the beginning; the white race from time immemorial had it. The class who were slaves had been elevated by degrees, taken out of the mud and mire, and now it is sought by their friends—although but four years have elapsed since they were submerged in the very slough of ignorance—to elevate them to the very stature and proportion of a free white, intellectual citizen. But the learned counsel says, "open the doors!" Open the doors for ignorance to associate with intellect; open the doors for the entrance of these elements that are so malleable in the hands of those who seek to use them! Open the doors for them who seek to control this government by numerical power! I deprecate in the name of my fellow-citizens, and in the name of humanity—nay, in the name of this very race itself—I deprecate such a result. Wait until they are fit. Wait until they have shown that they have the capacity for government before you place in their hands the very capstone of the edifice.

Section 1648 of the Code of Georgia says " among the rights of citizens are the enjoyment of personal security, of personal liberty, private property, and the disposition thereof, the elective franchise, the right to hold office, to appeal to the Courts, to testify as a witness, to perform any civil function, and to keep and bear arms."

When was that passed? It was when this country was a white man's country—when the white man alone was recognized as a citizen—when the capacity for self-government was supposed to exist only in the white race. The very Article from which it is taken went as far as the population of the State. First, stand citizens, highest in rank; second, aliens; third, persons of color—not as citizens, when this clause was originally adopted, but in the lowest grade of the population of the State. That Code was adopted then,

and it declared that "all citizens were entitled to exercise
all their rights, unless specially prohibited by law"—meaning what? That you could not prohibit citizens of one
grade or the other—the male white, the female white, the
infant white, the person of color—from the exercise of any
rights of citizenship which belong to their particular class.
It did not mean that you could not prohibit the white woman from voting or holding office; that you could not prohibit the white infant from voting or holding office; that
every right which belonged to each class of citizens could
not be taken from it, unless specially prohibited by law.

The laws state that infants and females shall not vote or
hold office. The Code says they cannot do it. They were
prohibited from exercising them. Now, how is it about the
persons of color? This clause as to the rights of citizens became the statute law of Georgia originally when there were
no persons holding office or able to hold office but white citizens. There were citizens of several kinds—male citizens,
female citizens, infant citizens. Then there were persons of
color, recognized by the Code as a lower portion. Now,
the Constitution of Georgia adopted this Code. And how?
It declares that in subordination only to the Constitution of
the United States and of the State of Georgia shall be:

"All acts passed by any legislative body, sitting in this
State as such since the 19th day of January, 1861, including that body of laws known as the Code of Georgia, and
the acts amendatory thereof, or passed since that time, which
said Code and acts are embodied in the printed book known
as "Irwin's Code;" and also so much of the Common and
Statute laws of England and of the Statute laws of Georgia,
as were in force in this State on the 19th day of December,
1860, as are not superseded by said Code, though not embodied therein, except so much of the said several Statutes, Code
and Laws as may be inconsistent with the supreme law
herein recognized, or may have been passed in aid of the
late rebellion against the United States, or may be obsolete,
or may refer to persons held in slavery, which excepted laws
are inoperative and void. * * * "

Now let us read Section 1661 of the Code, which that article of the Constitution adopted: "All negroes, mulattoes,
mestizoes, and their descendants, having one-eighth negro
or African blood in their veins, shall be known in this State
as persons of color." That does not come in conflict with
the Constitution of the United States, nor with that part of

the Constitution of Georgia which says that persons of color shall have the right to make and enforce contracts, to sue and be sued, &c.—a section prescribing what shall be the rights of persons of color—nowhere giving them the right to hold office. It was passed after they were free. So far as it did not give them the right to vote, it came in conflict with the Constitution, and therefore this section could not take it from them. But, the Constitution giving them nowhere the right to hold office, it does not conflict with it. This is a portion of the great scheme adopted by the Constitution itself which continues in force all portions of the Code not inconsistent with the Constitution. This is one portion of the Code. It is a portion of the matters on which they are legislating—*"in pari materia."* It relates to the *status* of the different classes of citizens. Now, I maintain that these portions of the Code, of which I have spoken, do not conflict either with the Constitution of Georgia or the Constitution of the United States, as I have endeavored to show your Honors.

These sections must be considered as one Act. They were all passed since the time of slavery. They must be reconciled: for the law with regard to the construction of statutes is, that you must make them all stand together, if you can. These do stand in harmony. The Legislature has adopted the Code, and with it these sections—the original law, passed at a time when negroes were not citizens. They have adopted another portion, passed when negroes became freemen. One portion says that among the rights of citizens shall be the right to vote. The Convention did not think that that gave it to the negro, so they gave it to him in the Constitution. The rights of persons of color are definitely and specifically given, and nowhere the right to hold office. The latter clause—the *causa altera* is more particular, and the former is more general; therefore, the latter circumscribes the former.

I refer your Honors to Dwarris on Statutes. He says: "The general words in one clause of a statute may be restrained by the particular words in the same clause of a statute." And, further, "As one part of a statute is properly called in to help the construction of another part, and is fitly so expounded as to support and give effect, if possible, to the whole; so is the comparison of one law with other laws made by the same Legislature, or upon the same subject, or relating expressly to the same point, enjoined for the same reason, and attended with a like advantage. In applying the maxims of interpretation, the object is throughout—first, to ascertain by legitimate means, and next, to carry into effect the object, of the framer."

Now, when the Constitution adopted this Code, what did it intend? To adopt these laws under the rules of the interpretation of Statutes—under the rule that all parts of these laws, as one or more statutes, should stand together, if possible. They were the framers, and that was their intention.

"It is, therefore," says Dwarris, an established rule of law that all acts *in pari materia* are to be taken together as if they were one law."

Here are two about citizens of different kinds. You must take them together. Both have been adopted by the Constitution, "and." Dwarris further says, "they are directed to be compared in the construction of statutes, because they are considered as framed upon one system and having one object in view."

"The 22 and 23 Car. 2, c. 10, for the better settling of intestates' estates, is continued, with some additional clauses, by the 1 Jac. 2 c. 17. It was holden by Lord Hardwicke, Chancellor, that for this reason the latter statute must be construed as if the former had been therein recited.

"Where acts are *in pari materia*, if the same word be used in both statutes, a distinction made in the one is a legislative exposition of the sense in which it is to be understood in the other."

Now, if you take both of these statutes as they stand: First, that the general rights of citizens are so and so, and then, that the rights of other citizens are so and so, how are you to do it unless the latter circumscribes the former? The rights of a citizen in his full superiority and capacity, the rights of a freeborn, educated, capable white citizen are one thing; and the rights of a citizen of the lower class—the class just taken from ignorance and vice, whose chains have just been stricken from their limbs—the rights to which they, in the eyes of the Legislature, are competent, and to which alone they can properly aspire, form another and quite a different thing. The rights to which free born, educated white male citizens are entitled, and to which they may aspire, are those mentioned in the first section; while those in the second are the rights to which the lower classes referred to, may aspire. You must take these two sections as a harmonious whole. Says Dwarris: "The intent of the

Legislature is not to be collected from any particular expression, but from a general view of the whole act of parliament." This Code is one whole act, made so by the adopting clause of the Constitution of Georgia. "Again, when in several statutes *in pari materia,* the Legislature is found sometimes inserting and sometimes omitting a clause of relation, it is to be presumed *that their attention has been drawn to the point, and that the omission is designed.*" This might be said to be such a case. We have first a section stating what shall be the rights of citizens, that is, the higher class of citizens. Further on we find legislation for another class of citizens; and the rule says, it is to be presumed that their attention has been drawn to the point, and they failed to change it.

It is not to be supposed that our legislators would elevate at one bound, without trial or experience, to the standard of the educated and capable white citizen, a class of persons just emerged from slavery. Having given them first the fundamental rights of citizens, and next the right to vote, they concluded that they had done all that was necessary and proper for them to do.

I respectfully submit to your Honors, in conclusion, that unless you can find in the Constitution or Statutes that *specific* or *express* grant to the negro, of the right to hold office, you cannot by *implication* clothe him with it; for all the implications are to the contrary—the implications of law, of reason, of common prudence, and of humanity.

ARGUMENT OF COL. AMOS T. AKERMAN.

Col. Akerman, for Plaintiff in Error, said:

May it Please your Honors:

The question is, are colored men eligible to office in Georgia?

There is nothing in the Constitution or statutes disqualifying them expressly. But it is argued on the other side that, having been disqualified under the ancient institutions of the State, they remain disqualified unless qualified by distinct and positive enactment. This argument ignores the revolutionary deluge which has swept over the land, and assumes that the ancient polity of the State is still our polity, that the present government is a continuation and not a new creation.

This assumption is a fundamental error. The authorities of the United States have twice declared that the war left Georgia without civil government, and these declarations have received the express or implied assent of all the people of the State. President Johnson's proclamation, of June 17th, 1865, and the Reconstruction Acts of 1867, both undertake to provide a government for a State which has none. The language of the proclamation is, "The rebellion in its revolutionary progress has deprived the people of Georgia of all civil government." The language of the Reconstruction Act of March 2d, 1867, is, "Whereas, no legal governments now exist in the rebel States of Georgia," &c. Both these instruments establish new bases of suffrage and eligibility for the Conventions which they authorize.

From these two sources have sprung the only State governments which have demanded the obedience of the people of Georgia since May, 1865, and one or the other of these governments has received the voluntary support of every citizen of the State. For in that warm popular conflict which began in March, 1867, and was formally terminated in January, 1869, by the abandonment of the suit brought by Governor Jenkins in the Supreme Court of the United States, every one of our citizens ranked himself among the adherents of the government initiated by the President, or among the adherents of the government initiated by Congress.

The Supreme Court of the United States is reported to have decided, in a late case, that the old government of

5

Mississippi was destroyed by the war, and the same must be true of Georgia. So, all the departments of the Government of the United States, and all the people of Georgia, have concurred in recognizing the destruction of the ancient government of the State. So complete was this destruction in the judgment of the Convention of 1865 and of that of 1867–8, that they thought it necessary to re-enact the body of our common and statute laws. There is a significance in current terms. We do not say that the government has been amended, repaired, or remodeled, but *reconstructed;* that is, wholly built anew. And the essential newness of the structure is not disproved by the fact that some of the old materials have been used. This reconstructed government being the authority under which this Court sits, I shall confine my inquiries to its rules and principles on the matter at bar. These must be sought for in the Constitution of 1868, and in the conformable statute law.

Looking at the Constitution, we find citizenship, and a certain age, residence and professional standing are required of those who shall fill a few specified offices; and for no other office is any qualification specially laid down. There are certain disqualifications for any office, to wit: unpardoned felony and larceny, holding public money unaccounted for, dueling, treason, embezzlement, malfeasance in office, bribery, idiocy and insanity. Neither European blood is made a qualification, nor African blood a disqualification. Black and white are words not found in the instrument. Under the maxim, the expression of some is the exclusion of others, it may be fairly argued that all are qualified who are not expressly disqualified. But it may be asked, whom do I mean by *all?* for no one can mean so absurd a thing as that all persons on earth, or in the State, not of the classes expressly disqualified, are eligible to office. I answer, all to whom political functions are given by the Constitution; all who act in matters pertaining to the government; all who in a strict political sense we denominate *the people.* And these are the *voters.* These constitute the political family. In these resides the sovereignty, if we have any such thing in this land. All public business is their business, and is done through agents only for convenience. These agents we style officers. These elementary truths are no where better expressed than by Mr. Webster, in one of his speeches in the Senate. "Government," says he, " is an agency created for the good of the people, and every person in office is the agent and servant of the people. Offices are created, not for the benefit of those who are to fill them, but for the public convenience."—Works, Vol. VI, page 183.

Now, it is unquestioned that colored men are voters in Georgia. Exercising that primary function, is it not according to reason that they should be eligible to the derivative functions, when not expressly disabled? In the absence of positive disqualifications, the right to vote includes eligibility to office; the capacity to select includes capacity to be selected; a capacity to be a principal includes a capacity to be an agent; a capacity to depute includes a capacity to be deputed. If colored men are part of the fountain, why are they not a part of the stream that flows from that fountain?

Of course, the people in framing a government may confine certain functions to a part of their body. When they have not done so, all the members of the political corporation are presumed to be equal in rights and franchises. The doctrine that suffrage includes eligibility is not new. It was recognized ages ago in the composition of the English House of Commons. "The capacity to elect and to be elected were originally considered the same, and used as convertible terms." Dwarris on Statutes, 190.

The learned Judge below places eligibility to office in a higher rank than suffrage. However correct this may be in the popular view, it is not correct in the view of the law. In the republican theory, an officer is above the people only as a wave is above the sea from which it rises, and to which it returns as soon as its brief prominence is over. The servant is not above his master. His Honor's view is derived, perhaps unconsciously, from European ideas. According to the monarchical theory, the sovereign gets his authority from Heaven, and all officers, being his representatives, and partaking in some sense of his superiority, are above the people among whom they officiate. Our officers derive their power not from a source above the people, but from the people themselves.

The learned Judge below argues against the doctrine that eligibility goes with suffrage—that it leads to the consequence that a foreigner who has declared his intention to become a citizen would be eligible to office; for such a foreigner can vote. The learned counsel on the other side (Mr. Hartridge) has pressed the same argument this morning with great earnestness, and pronounces such a consequence monstrous. That such is a consequence of the doctrine, I admit; but it does not frighten me. Seats in our executive and legislative chairs, and in our highest judiciary, are restricted to citizens by the terms of the Constitution. And in case of the minor offices, such as clerks, sheriffs and constables, if a man born abroad so commends himself to his neighbors here that with all their partialities for their own countrymen they will trust him in office after a short residence, I cannot believe he will endanger the State. The probability that a foreign power would endeavor to overturn our Government through such agencies is scarcely sufficient to require the rejection of a sound principle in order to escape that consequence.

Equality of right under this government is to be presumed in favor of all who participated equally in the formation of it—1 English (Ark.) Rep. 512. Colored men voted here on the queston whether there should be a Convention, and for delegates to the Convention; colored men sat in the Convention; colored men voted on the ratification of the Constitution.

The old government of Georgia was made exclusively by white men, and might properly be termed a "white man's government." Its primary franchises were restricted to white men. The present government was made by men of both races. Its primary franchise is bestowed without distinction of color. It was the genius of the old government that the white man should take everything by implication, and the negro nothing. It is the genius of this government that its implications should be without distinction of color. There, in the case of the colored man, privation of all rights, personal, civil, and political, was the rule; and possession of right was the exception. Here, participation in all rights is the rule, and privation is the exception.

The disabilities of the free negro under the old government grew out of the institution of slavery, and were a part of the bulwarks by which it was protected. Bryan vs. Walton, 14 Geo. Rep., 202. The cause ceasing, the effect should cease. When slavery fell, there fell also all the rights, members and appurtenances thereunto belonging. Why try to preserve the incidents when the principal thing has perished? Slavery has gone, with its rights of property and mastery, and its duties of protection; with its hardships and its mitigations: with its relations, sometimes forbidding, but often tender and affectionate; with its practices, sometimes harsh, but generally kind—much kinder, in fact, than a stranger would infer from the written law—and why should not its theory of political caste go too? If in good faith we have given it up, let us give it up totally. Having lost the substance in a fair and gallant fight, let us not cling to its appendages. Let us dismiss its jealousies, its apprehensions, its prejudices, its modes of thought, and its rules for interpreting constitutions. Its doctrines and spirit are out of place in a government based on liberty. If Georgia had never been a slave-holding State, and were now organized for the first time under this Constitution, this question would never have been raised. Shall a dead institution forever haunt us, and be allowed the privileges of the living?

It has been said that in adopting the old law of the State, the Constitution kept in force such of the old disabilities of colored persons as were not distinctly repealed. It will, however, be seen from the adopting clause, Article IX, section 3, that obsolete laws are excepted from the adoption. This clause was not in the Constitution of 1865, and was probably inserted with a view to the laws growing out of slavery, though not referring directly to slaves ; for the law of slavery is repealed in the next clause. It will be observed, too, that no such thing as the common law of Georgia is adopted, and many of the disablities of free colored persons rested alone on usage, which is, in fact, a common law. The common law adopted is that of England, which is against slavery and all its incidents. There is also a repeal of all law inconsistent with the Constitution, and I have endeavored to show that the Constitution authorizes no discrimination in political rights on account of race.

In the interesting argument for the defendant in error made this morning, (by Mr. Hartridge) we were told that among the rights now belonging to the negro, and first conferred by the Constitution of 1865, is the right to pursue the path of knowledge. That right is very restricted, if the old law in relation to free persons of color be law still where it has not been distinctly repealed. Where will you find a distinct repeal of the laws that forbid the instruction of that race? Perhaps in the Constitution of 1868, which provides for the education of all the children in the State. But that provision is thought by some to have spent itself in a mandate to the first Legislature which should assemble under that Constitution—a mandate which, unfortunately, has not been obeyed. And even if that provision is still in force so as to secure the right of receiving instruction, we remember that there was a law on our ancient statute book making it penal for a free negro to teach a free negro to read. Why is not this law still in force under the doctrine of the defendant in error that the ancient disabilities of free negroes are yet existing where not distinctly repealed? Under our doctrine that the present Constitution gives them every civil

and political right possessed by whites, the free negro can
be a teacher as well as a scholar, without hindrance from
the law, and we avoid the inhuman conclusion that a colored man is subject to imprisonment for instructing his own
race.

I come now to the question, What did the makers of our
Constitution understand it to mean upon the matter here in
issue? Says Chief Justice Taney, in the case of Dred Scott,
19 Howard 404: "The Constitution must be administered
according to its true intent and meaning when it was adopted." In the case of Padelford & Fay vs. The Mayor and
Aldermen of Savannah, 14 Ga. Rep., 454, the Supreme
Court of Georgia, through Judge Benning, says: "The Constitution, like every other instrument made by men, is to be
construed in the sense in which it was understood by the
makers of it at the time when they made it." To ascertain
that sense, the Court resorts to the debates in the Conventions and to the popular discussions of the times, quoting
both from the friends and opponents of the Constitution.
The same rules are applicable to the present inquiries.

In discussing events so recent as the formation of the
present Constitution of Georgia, we are under the disad-
vantage of touching the controversies of the hour. But we
also have the advantage of dealing with matters that have
happened within our own memory, and of access to abundant sources of information.

The makers of our Constitution were, first, the Convention that framed it; next, and perhaps most efficiently, the
people who ratified it; and finally, the Congress of the United States, which claimed the right of approving it before it
could become our fundamental law.

There was action on this subject in the Convention three
times. The report of the Committee on Franchise, after
prescribing who should vote and who should be disqualified
for office, contained the following provision, numbered as
the tenth section of the report: "All qualified electors, and
none others, shall be eligible to any office in this State, unless disqualified by the Constitution of this State, or by the
Constitution of the United States."—Journal, page 150. On
the 13th of February, 1868, a motion was made to amend
this section by inserting after the word "electors," the
words "who have been citizens of the United States for
seven years." It was well understood in the Convention
what was intended by this amendment. As colored persons
had just attained citizenship, it would debar them from
office for seven years. On this amendment the yeas were

thirty-three, and the nays eighty-nine.—Journal, pages 308-9. By that vote the Convention refused to impose a disqualification on colored men even for the limited term of seven years.

The next day the vote was taken on a motion to strike out the section altogether, and the yeas were one hundred and twenty-six and the nays were twelve.—Journal, pages 311-12. I will remark on this vote in a moment.

The next day, the 15th, a motion was made to reconsider this last vote, for the purpose of inserting as a substitute for the section the following:

"White men, only, shall be eligible to any office of trust, honor, or profit, or employment, whether municipal, judicial or political, in this State, and white men, only, shall serve as jurors in the Courts." On this motion the yeas were nineteen, the nays one hundred and three. Journal, pages 322-23.

So it stands upon the record thus: The Convention twice refused to deny eligibility to the colored man, and once refused specifically to give him eligibility. And the action latest in date was against denying him eligibility. But we are asked to account for the vote on the 14th of February, striking out the tenth section. As well as one can know the minds of other men, I know that a large majority of the members who voted to strike out the tenth section, did so under a conviction that it would be superfluous if it remained. It was not so with all; it was with the greater part, probably with all but the thirty-three who had voted to deny eligibility for seven years. Some of the members believed that eligibility was a derivative from citizenship; some that it was a derivative from suffrage; and some traced it to both these sources; probably three-fourths believed that it would exist as well without as with the tenth section. There was only one speech against the motion to strike out. The speaker thought it would be better to leave no chance for dispute or litigation upon the subject, and therefore opposed the motion. But he emphatically stated in his remarks, a synopsis of which appears in a newspaper of the day, that "it was well understood that a majority of the Convention held that negroes would be eligible to office even though that section were stricken out." This statement was gainsaid by nobody. It passed unchallenged in that body as the truth of the case.

The Constitution came before the people for ratification. There was full discussion by speakers and writers. Some of those who argue this case, and some of those are to decide it, engaged in these discussions. Your Honors understand that I refer to those discussions with no desire to bring into this forum the popular passions which then raged, but because the reference is necessary in order to ascertain what the people meant when they ratified the Constitution. Leading friends and leading opponents of the Constitution gave to the people their respective interpretations, andthese interpretations were accepted by their respective followers. And this is the way the parties stood before the people upon the subject now under discussion. The opponents of the Constitution all represented it as giving the negro the right to office. The large majority of the advocates of the Constitution gave it the same construction; a minority of its advocates, including some gentlemen of great eminence, held the contrary, but on every occasion candidly said to the people that there was a difference of opinion among the friends of the Constitution on this point; they took every precaution to let the people know that their construction was not unquestioned; they never denied that the majority of the Convention held to the opposite construction.

The formal attack on the Constitution was begun in this city of Atlanta, the day before the Convention adjourned. A gentleman who was exceedingly conspicuous in all the discussions upon the subject of reconstruction (Hon. Benjamin H. Hill) on that day addressed a meeting here, and, to use the current phrase, "laid down the programme" of opposition to the Constitution. In that speech, of March 10th, 1868, which was published in the Atlanta Daily Intelligencer of March 13th, 1868, Mr. Hill said, "I assert, and assert it without fear of contradiction, that this Constitution makes the negroes politically equal in all respects. It makes them equal as to the right of suffrage, and equal as to the right to hold office." From this position of their acknowledged leader, there was not a word of dissent expressed by the opponents of the Constitution, from that day until the ratifying election, which began on the 20th of April, 1868. Though of course I could not have heard all that was said, or have read all that was printed on the subject, I feel authorized to make this statement, from a very vivid recollection of the discussion preceding that election.

It may be safely assumed that the masses of the people were divided on this question in about the same proportions as their leaders. They would then stand as follows in round numbers: The seventy-one thousand who voted against ratification (but who having voted at the election, are bound by it) voted with the understanding that the Constitution made colored men eligible. Of the eighty-nine thousand who voted for ratification, the large majority, probably three-fourths, voted with the same understanding. Thus, as near as can ascertained, about one hundred and forty thousand voters at that election agreed to the construction that makes colored men eligible, and about twenty thousand considered them ineligible.

The action of the people in the choice of officers at the same election at which the Constitution was ratified, proves that the colored men were generally supposed to be eligible. They were candidates for office whenever they chose to be, and many of them were elected and peaceably entered on their offices. In the enlightened county of Chatham, the very party who brings up this case was chosen at that election. If there had been any serious doubt of their eligibility, it is not at all probable that so many of them would have sought or received an election.

Thus we have, so far as such things are ascertainable, the sense of the Convention and of the people. Congress has not made any positive declaration on the subject. The Constitution was approved generally by an act passed June 25, 1868. But the only difficulty in Congress with regard to the reconstructed States has occurred in the case of Georgia, and it is well known that much of that difficulty has grown out of the exclusion of colored members from our legislative bodies. Hence it may be inferred that the Congress which ratified the Constitution construed it in the same way as the Convention which framed it and the majority of the people who ratified it.

If the right of eligibility were not established by the foregoing considerations, it would still exist by our statute defining the rights of citizens, as has been well shown by my associate counsel (Col. Stone.) The Constitution adopts the Code as our statute law until repealed. The Code, paragraphs 1648, 1650 and 1651, declares that eligibility to office is among the rights of citizens of the lawful age, sex, and other prescribed qualifications.

It is due to truth to say that these paragraphs were not adverted to in the Convention, or in the popular discussion of which I have spoken until late in the canvass. Then, attention was drawn to them, and it is well known that some intelligent men who had supposed this right not to be given in the Constitution, became convinced that it was given in the statute law which the Constitution adopted.

An ingenious attempt has been made to prove that the

obvious meaning of those paragraphs is not the true meaning. The learned counsel (Mr. Hartridge) shows that in another place the Code defines persons of color and gives to
them certain civil rights—whence he infers that, being thus
specially provided for, the rights enumerated as belonging
to citizens generally do not belong to them. In support of
this view, he cites certain rules of construction from Dwarris. Such rules are useful in ascertaining the meaning of
what is not plain. But the force of language so plain and
positive as that used in those paragraphs cannot be overcome by any such process. It will be difficult to convince
the Court that the colored man acquired no new privileges
by becoming a citizen.

His Honor below argues that eligibility cannot be included in citizenship, because in that case women and children would be eligible. He does not see that citizens of
different descriptions may have different rights, and yet
have them all by virtue of their citizenship. I will read on
this subject from 1st Littell's Ky. Reports, page 333–4:
"No one can therefore, in the correct sense of the term, be
a citizen of a State, who is not entitled, upon the terms prescribed by the institutions of the State, to all the rights and
privileges conferred by these institutions upon the highest
class of society. It is true that females and infants do not
personally possess those rights and privileges in any State in
the Union; but they are generally dependent upon adult
males, through whom they enjoy the benefits of those rights
and privileges. And it is a rule of common law, as well as
of common sense, that females and infants in this respect
partake of the quality of those adult males who belong to
the same class and condition in society." According to the
rule here laid down, the act which makes new citizens may
clothe them with different privileges according to age, sex
and other conditions.

What are the rights of citizens? Every mind directed to
the subject must have found this a perplexing question. I
doubt whether an accurate and exhaustive definition of the
term citizen has ever been framed. The Court below undertook to define it negatively, a much easier task than to define
it positively. Counsel on the other side cited numerous authorities to prove that the privileges and immunities of citizens of each State, to be enjoyed in other States, under the
Constitution of the United States, embrace only certain personal and civil rights. But this has not been held uniformly,
as the case I have quoted from Kentucky shows. The Court
below argues that the privileges guaranteed to citizens in

the Fourteenth Amendment to the Constitution must be the same for all citizens without regard to age, sex or condition, and hence that eligibility to office cannot be one of them, because that construction would open office to women and children. This mode of reasoning would fritter to nothing the privileges secured in that instrument. Is the right of locomotion one of these privileges? This right is abridged in the cases of children, lunatics, criminals, and in some instances, of debtors. Is the right to contract one of them? This right is abridged in the cases of minors, married women, and other incapacitated classes. It will scarcely be asserted that the States, in imposing these salutary restraints, are violating the Constitution of the United States.

We remember when it was the fashion among Southern jurists who were defending the laws forbidding the immigration of free colored persons against constitutional objections, to contend that citizens were the highest class of persons in their respective States, and as free colored persons were under some disabilities in most Northern States, they could not be held citizens in the sense of the Constitution of the United States. This was the view taken by the Kentucky Court, in the case in 1st Littell. Now, in order to restrict the privileges of colored persons under their new citizenship, our learned friends place the citizen very low in the scale of privilege.

Perhaps it is the true solution of the perplexity that the word means different things in different places. There is respectable authority for limiting it, as used in the Constitution of the United States, to personal and civil rights. There is respectable authority for saying that it sometimes embraces the rights of suffrage and eligibility to office.— 1st Litt. 333 ; Bouvier, Law Dict. Art. Citizen ; 1st Bouv. Inst. 64.

It may be profitable to inquire how the term has been understood in Georgia. Though there has been " a solution of continuity" between the former and the present governments of the State, the old may yet, in many particulars, afford valuable aid in understanding the new. It will be seen that men whom Georgians have been accustomed to revere believed that citizenship in Georgia carried with it the right to hold office in the absence of positive restrictions.

On the 13th of February, 1796, an act of the Legislature of Georgia was passed with the assent of Jared Irwin, Gov-

ernor, freeing certain slaves of Daniel Grant and also Cha-
ney and her nine children. It enacts that the freed persons
" are hereby emancipated, freed and enabled to take, hold
and enjoy property of every kind in like manner as if they
were free citizens of this State." At the end of the act it is
" provided, nevertheless, that nothing herein contained shall
extend, or be construed to extend, to entitle the said free
mulatoes and negro slaves, when liberated as aforesaid, to
serve as jurors in any case whatsoever, or to render them, or
either of them competent witnesses in any cause or case
where the personal rights or property of any white person
or persons is or are concerned, *or to entitle them, or any of
them, to have or hold, directly or indirectly, any office of trust
or profit, civil or military, within this State."*

On the 2d of December, 1799, an act was passed with the
assent of Governor Jackson, entitled " An act to admit
James Stewart and Judy Eltof, free persons of color, to the
privileges of free citizens of this State as far as is therein
expressed." Precisely the same provision is made in the
case of the man James Stewart as those which I have quoted
from the other acts. But observe how carefully these acts
were drawn. The section which relates to the woman Judy
does not expressly deny her the right to hold office, because
her sex would exclude her. It is in these words: " And
whereas, Judy Eltof, a free person of color, has petitioned this
Legislature to be made a free citizen of this State ; Be it
therefore enacted, That the said Judy Eltof, of the county of
Richmond, be, and she is hereby vested with and entitled
to all the rights, privileges and immunities belonging to a
free citizen of this State, with this exception, that she shall
not be a competent witness in any case where the personal
rights or property of any white person may be concerned."
These acts may be found in Marbury and Crawford's Digest,
pages 204, *et seq.* The careful legislators of that day considered that even free negroes, when made citizens, would
thereby become eligible to office unless expressly prohibited,
and hence they inserted these precautionary provisos. More
recently we find one of the most enlightened and cultivated
men in the State expressing the same opinion. In 1848, the
late R. M. Charlton, in arguing the case of *Cooper & Worsham, vs. The Mayor, &c., of Savannah,* contended that if
colored persons were citizens, they might represent us in
the Legislature.—4 Georgia Reports, 41.

I am, therefore, well sustained in the position that in

Georgia citizenship, in the cases of adult males, white or colored, has been usually understood to involve the right of eligibility to office.

I have had notice that the counsel who will follow me for the defendant in error will read the act of Congress conferring the right to office on colored men in the District of Columbia, and the argument will be made that Congress did not believe that the right to office was included in the citizenship and suffrage which had been previously bestowed. My answer is, first, this act was passed before the ratification of the Fourteenth Amendment to the Constitution of the United States; second, Congress might have thought it better to cut short a controversy by an act, strictly unnecessary, than to leave open so agitating a question, especially in that District, where the old law of Maryland discriminating against the blacks might be still living in the prejudices of some of the people.

The argument has been made, and I think it a sound one, that the right to hold office not being given in the Constitution to the white man by name any more than to the black man by name, the black man, therefore, stands on the same footing as the white. To this it has been replied that eligibility to office is the white man's birthright. I cannot comprehend the notion of a birthright to office under a government like ours, where office is not a privilege of the holder, but a trust for the benefit of others, which they may confer or withhold at pleasure. Further, I cannot see how a man can have a birthright in a government which did not come into existence until long after he was born.

Counsel on the other side draw an argument from the acts of Congress. I am at liberty, therefore, to draw an argument from the acts of other departments of the government of the United States. The Constitution of the United States is as silent on the subject of race or color as the Constitution of Georgia. Yet the late President (Johnson) and the present President (Grant) have appointed colored men to office. The United States Senate—a body comprising much legal learning—has confirmed nominations of colored men. If colored men can hold office under the Constitution of the United States, they can do so under the Constitution of Georgia. In either case they are *our* officers—that is, our agents.

The learned counsel on the other side (Mr. Hartridge) has told us that "it is not to be presumed that the Convention, without trial and without experience of the capacity of the colored man to fill office, would elevate him to that right."

He should have remembered that colored men had trial and experience in public business as registers of voters for the Convention and as members of the Convention. And let me ask, with all respect, when will colored men have office, if they must be excluded until they are tried and experienced in it? One will not learn to swim by staying out of the water.

In the same strain, counsel has urged upon your Honors the improbability that the makers of the Constitution would open office to men so ignorant as most colored men are. No such improbability exists. The makers of the present Constitution were no more afraid of ignorance in office than their predecessors—the makers of our earlier Constitutions. Neither the Constitution of the United States nor the Constitution of Georgia has ever made ignorance a disqualification for the highest office. What law has there been since 1789 to prevent the most ignorant citizen in the land, of the lawful age and birth, from being President? What has there been to prevent the greatest dunce in Georgia, of the proper age and citizenship, from being Governor or sitting in the Legislature? The learned counsel cannot believe that the Convention would give to "those lately submerged in the slough of ignorance those rights which the free-born, educated white man may aspire to." Aspirations to office have never been limited by law to the educated. The Convention has given to colored men no rights but those which the most uneducated, most ignorant, and most stupid white man has always been at liberty to aspire to. Why is ignorance now, for the first time, so alarming? Is it not as dangerous under a white skin as under a black skin? Gentlemen seem to apprehend that if the colored man has a right to office, he will certainly get it, however unfit he may be. This fear is groundless.

In the first place, it is not to be presumed, from our past history, that the incapable will aspire; and in the next place, it is not to be presumed that those who are fit to select will make a bad selection.

Our Presidents, Governors and Legislators have been intelligent men, though there has been no law to exclude the ignorant from those high seats. The modesty which has checked the aspirations of ignorant blacks; or, if that should fail, the elective body will, from a sense of its own interests, repress incapacity into its natural place. In a republican government it must always be possible for the people to vote foolishly. Yet, republican government rests on the supposition that the people will vote wisely in the main.

That discretion may sometimes be abused, is not a sufficient reason for denying discretion altogether. It need not be feared that many colored men will get office, unless they prove themselves competent for it. The Convention probably thought that ignorant blacks could be risked where ignorant whites had been risked so long and so safely.

Counsel says that the Code was made when this was a white man's country. No matter when the Code was made. It is the law for us now, by virtue of its adoption in the Constitution. No matter whose the country was when the Code was made. It is now the country of every citizen in it—the country of the white man and of the black man together. They are bound together politically by a common fortune. The prosperity that visits the one will bless the other. The calamity that injures the one will afflict the other. Here they must both live. Here they must both labor. Here they may both vote. And here, if I am right in this argument, either may hold office when his fellow-citizens choose to trust him with office. As they are one in interest and one in destiny, I do not believe that the State will suffer harm from having made them one in political right.

ARGUMENT OF MR. LLOYD.

MR. THOMAS E. LLOYD, Counsel for Defendant in Error, said:

MAY IT PLEASE THE COURT:

I desire at the outset to make some few observations in reference to the preliminary points in this case.

The first point to which I shall call your Honors' attention is the fact that in the Court below the opening and conclusion was given to the Relator in this case. I apprehend that the judgment, the ruling, of the Court below, on that point, was perfectly correct. The Demurrer—I care not whether in the first or second instance—had been withdrawn. Now, having been called on to show cause, if the original demurrer had stood, the party may have been considered the *promovent* in the case; but when he had filed his plea, when he had joined issue, in which we had taken the affirmative and he the negative—in which we stated that he had one-eighth or more of negro blood in his veins, and he denied it, then the relative positions were changed We were the *promovents*. The burden of proof of the whole cause rested upon us, and therefore were we entitled to the conclusion. The truth is, however, that if this matter had been argued regularly, the argument on the demurrer would not have been had until after the jury trial had been finished, because the party had put himself on the direct issue. He had denied having one-eighth negro blood in his veins: upon that, issue was joined, and upon that issue a continuance was asked for and granted, and a jury summoned to try it. If your Honors' will recall the case (in 4th Georgia) of The State against Green, you will remember that there the matter of fact was first tried. And why? Because, if the party had failed in proving that the plaintiff in error in this case had one-eighth negro blood in his veins, there would then have been no necessity for all this argument; and therefore, where a matter of fact is set forth in return to a writ of *Quo Warranto*, and issue is joined on that fact, that issue must first be tried, and when the fact is found, whether one way or the other, by the jury, then comes the judgement of the Court. That should have been the regular proceeding in this instance. The jury should have gone on and found the fact, whether or not the plaintiff in error, in this case, had one-eighth or more of negro or African blood in him. Then properly comes the argument, whether or not the Court would grant this writ of *Quo Warranto* against him, and then, when the argument would have come on in its regular way, we, being the *promovents*, would unquestionably have been entitled to the opening and conclusion.

Now, the only difference is, that instead of arguing after the issue of fact had been tried by the jury, we went on with the argument at once. We merely tried the legal question first: and that does not change the position which we occupied. We were still the *promovents*. We could not be anything else after the issue was joined. Up to the time of the joining of the issue, the party might perhaps have become the *promovent* by making certain objections, but afterwards our *status* was fixed: we were the *promovents* in the case, and entitled to open and conclude. But, as in a *mandamus* case, we ought to have argued the issue first, and that, if found in favor of the party, would have decided the whole matter, and there would have been an end of it. There would have been nothing for the Judge to decide. According to the statements of Counsel for the Plaintiff in Error, when the rule was granted to show cause why the writ of *Quo Warranto* should not issue, he filed a Demurrer. Then he was *promovent* in the case; but the very moment his Demurrer was withdrawn, and his plea filed, denying facts which we *asserted*, then we became *promovents*, and were entitled to open and conclude.

So far as the testimony of Mr. Jackson is concerned, the Court allowed it to go to the jury for what it was worth. The *status* of individuals may be proved by general reputation. It may be very difficult, in cases of this kind, to ascertain it in any other way than by general reputation.

With reference to the other testimony, as, for instance, these matters at the Court House, it appears by the testimony that these lists were posted up three weeks before the election. It appears that during this time White was there. He was elected at that time to the office from which we seek to displace him, and from which he has been displaced by judgment of the Court below. It was therefore submitted to the jury whether or not, under these circumstances when it was proved that he was one of the candidates, and that these lists were there for four or five weeks—whether it was not probable that he had seen them, and, if he had, whether it was not inference against him that he had failed to correct them.

The admission of the life insurance testimony is also objected to. Here is what the Bill of Exceptions of the Plaintiff in Error states in reference to it:

"The plaintiff introduced the witness, Howard, who testified that a certain book was a record book of an insurance company that had recorded in it an application for a policy from R. W. White; that the original application had, after record, been sent to New York, where it then was; that the original was truly copied in said book; that he did not know who presented said application; that he did not see Defendant sign it, nor did he know Defendant's hand-writing. The plaintiff offered to read said copy in said insurance book in evidence, and the Defendant objected."

Now, counsel said he would object to this, even if we had
6

had the original, on the ground, I suppose, that there is no evidence that the plaintiff in error signed it; but if the thing was made for him—if a Policy for R. W. White was made at all—I care not who signed it. It was recorded as an application for a policy from R. W. White, made upon the Knickerbocker Insurance Company of New York, and we have the testimony of Dr. Yonge that he did examine White as an applicant for a policy of insurance from that company. Is not that sufficient to identify the original, and to identify the man? This was a certified copy, and it was proved that the original was in New York, and out of our jurisdiction.

The rule of law unquestionably is that we must produce the original record, if we can get it; but what right can the Court give us to get a paper from New York? We may issue a commission and effect all that may be necessary; and I think the Supreme Court of this State decided, in a case which I do not now recollect, where a deed came up in Florida, that the witness was allowed to prove the handwriting of the writer. The Court said that that would be allowed, inasmuch as this Court did not know whether the laws of Florida required the witness to testify. Counsel says we did not show diligence towards procuring the original document. Where was the necessity of going through these mere formalities in order to obtain it, when the clear provisions of the law allow of its being done without that necessity? I maintain that the thing is sufficiently identified as an application for a Policy of Insurance which this man made; that the identification is accomplished by the testimony of Howard, as set forth in the Bill of Exceptions; and also by the fact that Dr. Yonge himself made an examination of the plaintiff in error for the Knickerbocker Insurance Company.

One word with reference to the charge of the Court. The counsel on the other side required the Court to charge that the party, the Relator in the case, must make out every point of his case. A charge of that kind may be calculated to mislead the jury; as, for instance, if we sought to prove a fact by a witness, and that witness failed to prove it. A charge of the kind would, therefore, mislead the jury as to the nature of the proof which was required before we could recover.

But the Court did charge in effect exactly what the motion requested. There was but one issue, and that was whether White had or had not one-eighth negro blood in his veins. That was all we undertook to prove, all we required

to prove, and all we could prove. The Court, in the charge
to the jury, says that we must prove that, and that the jury
must be satisfied of it. That was exactly what the counsel
desired, except that the Court gave it specifically. The counsel say we should make out our case in *every* particular.
The Court charged the jury that we must make it out in
that particular, and they must so find before they give us a
verdict. When the Court did that, he did everything desired by the counsel, merely changing the mode of its pre-
sentation.

Having thus premised, I will now proceed to examine the
main question of the case.

I must, however, take a different view of this matter to
that taken by counsel for the plaintiff in error. One of
them says we must look upon the Georgia of *ante bellum*
days as having been entirely blotted out. I am not here to
argue the very delicate question of the *status* of Georgia
for the past few years, nor as to whether we have been
States or Territories, or whether we have or have not been
a conquered people. Whatever our position, we have been
in one way or another at the mercy of the General Government. Were it necessary for us to be States, we were States;
were it necessary for us to be Territories, we were Territories; if it were necessary to have us otherwise, we were otherwise. Yet I cannot agree with the learned counsel that
the Georgia of the past is gone; that her history and her
institutions were utterly and absolutely destroyed by the
revolution which ended in 1865.

I am not disposed so to believe, because I do not think it
has been so held. Indeed, the State of Georgia, before this
present Constitution was drafted or adopted, had been called
upon by the government of the United States to do acts as
a State which she could do only as a State. Her position
as a State has been recognized.

When the act was passed which abolished slavery throughout the United States, and which enacted that slavery should
not hereafter exist, it was sent to the Legislature of the State
of Georgia for ratification; *and it was ratified by that Legislature*, and the ratification of that Legislature was the ratification of one of the States that was part and parcel of the
Constitution.

There are many points indicating that the State has not
been destroyed. Reconstructed, I grant you; changed in its
institutions, I grant you; modified to a great extent, I grant
you; the rights of some of its inhabitants taken away, and
the rights of others increased, I grant you: but, I still say

that Georgia is Georgia—except in so far as the hands of power have "reconstructed" her. I do not believe that we were blotted out of existence. I do not think we began a new era, and that we should blot out our history and speak of this as the fourth year of the existence of Georgia. We are still the State of Georgia—call it "in rebellion" if you will—but still the State of Georgia; a State and a community, having institutions at the time the war closed, which institutions however the General Government had modified. I have therefore, in arguing this question, the right to say that the *substratum* of Georgia still exists. The United States Government—to which we must all look now—the United States Congress, which is now supreme and which controls everything, has looked at it in the same way. I shall therefore argue this question upon this ground. How far has the legislation of Congress, the formation of this Constitution, and the legislation under it, changed the *status* of our people, and how far have they changed the status of the free person of color so as to give him the right to hold office? I say they have made no such change.

The Fourteenth Amendment to the Constitution of the United States says:

"All persons born or naturalized in the United States, and subject to the jurisdiction thereof, are citizens of the United States and of the State wherein they reside. No State shall make or inforce any law which shall abridge the privileges or immunities of citizens of the United States; nor shall any State deprive any person of life, liberty or property without due process of law, nor deny to any person within its jurisdiction, the equal protection of the laws."

The provision of our State Constitution bearing on citizenship is in almost precisely the same words. By these sections persons of color were made citizens. It was not intended to make white persons citizens, for they were already such. They were citizens by reason of their birthright—their inheritance. They were such from the time the State was settled; and they had from time immemorial exercised the privileges of citizenship. Who then were intended to be made citizens by the sections I have quoted? The colored people, unquestionably. They had not heretofore had any rights as such. They were not citizens, as is shown in 4th Georgia. They were, therefore, the class that were made citizens. The others had always been so. The question then is, to what extent were they so made citizens?

In arguing this question, we must look to the condition of the country at the time; and we must see from corresponding legislation—from what has been done by the United States Government itself—how they regarded this class of people. They have by their own course intimated to us and the Courts, what they think of the mode in which citizenship should be meted out to these parties.

Your Honors must consider the condition of this State, in connection with this matter; and although I know very little of politics, yet, I apprehend, there must be some political consideration—or rather not a political consideration, but an observation of the field of politics—must be expected to enter into your decision in this case. Here were four millions of persons who had, up to this time, been uninstructed; they had not been allowed to acquire education. With very few exceptions they were most ignorant. The legislation in behalf of these colored persons could not, however, be said to be legislation solely for the few of them who were intelligent; it was rather legislation for four millions of ignorant people.

The counsel says that there are large numbers of white people who are unfit for office. This is undoubtedly true, and it is much to be deplored. Still, they have had the benefits of education, as a class; and, having so long exercised the rights and privileges of citizenship, it is to be expected that they can continue to do so with ease and advantage. Here, however, were persons who had never exercised the privileges of citizenship until flung to them by the fortunes of war. Counsel says that it is to be presumed that at the time of emancipation, in the year 1865, the whole system of the Southern States was done away with; and that a new community rose up in its place! That is not so. I will not impute to any Convention, or any other body of intelligent men, that they had any such object in view, as that this great mass of ignorance should at one bound be lifted up to positions of control. It is well known that there are counties in Georgia where the colored population have the entire control. Was it to be expected that they, ignorant as they are and in the condition in which they were described in 14th Georgia Reports, uneducated and incapable, should be lifted at once to the privilege of governing counties and municipalities?

The gentlemen on the other side may know more about the Convention of 1867 8 than I do. My knowledge is derived solely from the books. I take the Journal of the Convention and the Constitution, and I examine them, and I draw, what I deem to be, an irresistible inference, that the Convention never intended to confer on colored persons the rights here claimed for them.

The Convention makes them citizens. Counsel says it is not easy to define the word "citizen." I will give your Honors, a clear, plain and simple definition of the word. I read from 19 Howard's Reports, page 422 :

"Undoubtedly, a person may be a citizen, that is a member of the community who form the sovereignty, although he exercises no share of the political power, and is incapacitated from holding particular offices. Women and minors, who form a part of the political family, cannot vote ; and when a property qualification is required to vote or hold a particular office, those who have not the necessary qualification cannot vote or hold office, yet they are citizens.

"So, too, a person may be entitled to vote by the laws of the State, who is not a citizen even of the State itself ; and in some of the States of the Union foreigners not naturalized are allowed to vote. And the State may give the right to free negroes and mulattoes, but that does not make them citizens of the State, and still less of the United States ; and the provision in the Constitution giving them the privileges and immunities in other States, does not apply to them."

I will now read from 4th Washington's Circuit Court Reports, page 381 :

"The right of a citizen of one State to pass through, or to reside in any other State, for the purposes of trade, agriculture, professional pursuits, or otherwise ; to claim the benefit of the writ of *habeas corpus ;* to institute and maintain actions of any kind in the courts of the State ; to take, hold and dispose of property, either real or peasonal ; and an exemption from higher taxes or impositions than are paid by the other citizens of the State ; may be mentioned as some of the particular privileges and immunities of citizens, which are clearly embraced by the general description of privileges deemed to be fundamental ; to which may be added the elective franchise, as regulated and established by the laws or Constitution of the State in which it is to be exercised."

These are the fundamental principles, and when a man comes to be a citizen, it does not necessarily imply that he has the right to vote or to hold office. These are not *necessary* rights of citizenship. In England, by the late Reform Bill, they have added a great deal to the number of those who had the right to vote; and England is to-day, to all intents and purposes, as free as our country; and yet there are large masses there who have always been citizens, but who, until within a year or two, never had the right to vote. The franchise has been frequently enlarged there. In 1832 the government of England was shaken to its centre and nearly revolutionized by the Reform Bill of that year. Later efforts to enlarge the franchise have been successfully made, and so it may go on until they get universal suffrage. The fact is undeniable, however, that there are to-day thousands of persons in Great Britain who cannot even vote, yet are citizens.

Upon the matter of education, to which extended reference has been made by counsel on the other side, *that* was implied in their freedom—liberty of action and freedom of thought were necessary accompaniments of their emancipation.

Now, may it please the Court, I hold that prior to the time of the revolution these persons of color had as distinct and specific a *status* in Georgia as any other class of persons. Neither by birthright, inheritance or otherwise did they have any rights other than those entirely fundamental in their character; and never was such a thing thought of as granting to them any such privileges as are claimed here. When they were emancipated, and were made citizens, they were made citizens of a lower grade. Reason and justice will bear me out in that assertion. They were given control of themselves, and of their property; of the disposition of their own time, and the protection of their person. That is the grade of citizenship conferred by this Constitution.

The Constitution of this State says: "All persons born or naturalized in the United States, and resident in this State, are hereby declared citizens of this State, and no law shall be made or enforced which shall abridge the privileges or immunities of citizens of the United States or of this State, or deny to any person within its jurisdiction the equal protection of its laws."

After thus making colored persons citizens, it goes on to say who shall have the right to vote; who shall be deemed electors. It does not simply say that "naturalized citizens shall have the right to vote," nor that "persons who have declared their intention" to become such shall have the right to vote. That might leave the right of the colored man

doubtful. It goes on to say, however, that "*Every male*
person born in the United States, and every male person
who has been naturalized, or who has legally declared his
intention to become a citizen of the United States, twenty-one
years old or upwards, who shall have resided in this State
six months next preceding the election, and shall have resided thirty days in the county in which he offers to vote,
and shall have paid all taxes which may have been required
of him, and which he may have had an opportunity of paying agreeably to law, for the year next preceding the election, (except as hereinafter provided,) who may be a resident
of the State at the time of the adoption of this Constitution
shall be deemed an elector as aforesaid."

Why does the Constitution come out so much in detail,
so plainly, and so specifically on that point? Evidently
because the makers of it did not hold that citizenship of
itself conferred the right to vote.

Let me now read the celebrated 10th section, which was
intended to give to the colored man the right to hold office:

" All qualified electors, and none others, shall be eligible
to office in this State, unless disqualified by the Constitution
of this State, or by the Constitution of the United States."

That would undoubtedly have given to the colored man
the right to hold office; but the Convention refused to adopt
it.

Beginning with emancipation, the rights of a freeman
have been gradually given to the colored man. They ought
to have been given gradually, and they were so given.

If my argument on this question is correct, that the mere
fact of being a citizen does not carry with it the right to vote
or hold office, we will find by observation and examination
of the Constitution that the class of people of whom we are
speaking have had the right to vote conferred upon them in
this State and in the United States; and we will find by an
examination of the acts of the United States Congress, that
a special law of that body was deemed necessary in order
to enable colored people to vote in the District of Columbia.
I read from the United States statutes of 1866-7, page 375."

" *Be it enacted by the Senate and House of Representatives
of the United States of America in Congress assembled*, That
from and after the passage of this act, each and every male
person, excepting paupers and persons under guardianship,

of the age of twenty-one years and upwards, who has not been convicted of any infamous crime or offence, and accepting persons who may have voluntarily given aid or comfort to the rebels in the late rebellion, and who shall have been born or naturalized in the United States, and who shall have resided in the said District for the period of one year, and three months in the ward or election precinct in which he offers to vote, next preceding any election therein, shall be entitled to the elective franchise, and shall be deemed an elector and entitled to vote at any election in said District, without any distiction on account of color or race."

These parties had been emancipated and I think made citizens. Congress had exclusive control over the District of Columbia, and Congress was evidently of opinion that the citizenship of these people did not give them the right to vote. Hence, they conferred it upon them.

I will now read from another act of Congress of date 28th May, 1868, which goes further than the one just read. It is as follows:

"SEC. 2. *And be it further enacted*, That it shall be the duty of the Mayor of the City of Washington, District of Columbia, the Board of Aldermen, and the Board of Common Council thereof, to assemble in joint convention at the City Hall, in said city, on the first Tuesday in July, eighteen hundred and sixty-eight, and proceed to select by ballot, all officers whose appointments, upon the nomination of the Mayor, are now authorized by the charter, or by any law of the United States, or act or ordinance of said city, or which may hereafter be authorized thereby, and who shall hold their offices respectively for one year, and until a successor is appointed; and on the same day of the month in each year thereafter the joint convention shall proceed to a new selection; *Provided*, That no person shall be regarded as incompetent to hold any of said offices, or be disqualified therefor, who is a qualified elector in said District."

Your Honors will perceive that these matters have been entirely progressive; these parties having had conferred upon them first citizenship, then the right to vote, and next, as will be seen by the quotation which I just read, the right to hold office in the District of Columbia.

I therefore hold that the clauses in this Constitution which makes them citizens, does not give them the right to hold office. And, although the counsel may not think that we shall be overrun by foreigners holding civil appointments among us, yet it is contrary to the genius of any country to have parties holding office within her limits who are not her own citizens. It is a serious matter that parties should be allowed to hold offices of honor and profit and responsibility who are not even citizens of the country. Was it not then the sole object and intent of the Constitution to declare these people electors, and nothing more? The Convention could certainly not have intended anything else. There is nothing included in the word "citizen" which necessarily involves the right of suffrage or of office holding. If that be so, and the Constitution does not confer the right to hold office—what does? Do the statutes? I say no. Let us read the 3d section of article 11 of the Constitution of Georgia. It says that next to, and in subordination to, the Constitution of the United States and of this State, the laws in general force in this State shall be—

"All acts passed by any Legislative body sitting in this State as such, since the 19th day of January, 1861, including that body of laws known as the 'Code of Georgia' and the acts amendatory thereto."

Your Honors will find upon examination that this Code referred to was made in 1860. The section bearing upon persons of color was passed in 1866, and that, by the special provision of the Constitution which I have quoted, is re-adopted and re-affirmed by the present Constitution. The same section excepts from adoption all laws which "may refer to persons held in slavery."

The Code was adopted as the Legislature passed it—as a whole—making only a few specific exceptions. When the Legislature passed the section which says that all citizens shall be entitled to hold office, and the other section which says that all citizens are entitled to the exercise of all their rights as such unless specially prohibited by law, they also, and at the same time, passed a section which says that free persons of color are not of that class. When looking for the meaning of these sections, we must not look to the Convention, but to the Legislature which originally passed these laws. The Convention merely re-adopted what had already been adopted.

The Legislature of 1865-6 passed the section giving certain rights to persons of color, and when construing all these sections you must construe them together. They form, as it were, parts of one Act, and must, according to the rule of interpretation, be made to stand together if possible. The clause of the new Constitution re-adopting "that body of laws known as Irwin's Code," treated them as portions of one Act. In interpreting these sections we might go back to the history of the Legislature which first passed them, and of the Convention which re-adopted them. But the best way to interpret a statute or Constitution is to place one's self in the position of the law-makers, and endeavor to find out what they intended. Did the law-makers of 1866, when the section relating to citizens holding office was passed, mean that negroes should hold office? Not at all. Did the act of 1866 do so, which said that "persons of color shall have the right to make and enforce contracts," &c.? It did not. It gave them the first grade only of citizenship. It gave them the right to life, liberty and property. The Convention *adopted these laws*. The Convention went further, and enacted that they shall have the right to vote; but certainly does not give them the right to hold office—*expressio unius est exclusio alterius*. All these sections harmonize. They convey their sense plainly. Citizenship, with them, means the right to life, liberty and property, and embraces only fundamental principles. Take the Constitution and the Code, and refer to the Dred-Scott Decision, rendered by the Supreme Court of the United States, and consult Dwarris on statutes, and you will find my argument fully sustained. Disturb neither the Constitution nor the Code; make their provisions stand together; harmonize them according to the rule; give them such a construction as will reconcile them, the one with the other, and this conclusion is inevitable.

Dwarris says: "Where a general act of Parliament confers immunities which expressly exempts persons from the effect and operations of its provisions, it excludes all exemptions to which the subject might have been before entitled at common law. The introduction of the exemption is necessarily exclusive of all other independent extrinsic exemptions. The maxim is clear, '*expressum facit cessare tacitum*.' Affirmative specification excludes implication." The Convention has superadded the right to vote, but did *not* superadd the right to hold office; and nothing in in the Constitution of the United States, nor in the Constitution or laws of this State, confers upon persons of color any such right. If the mere fact of their becoming citizens gives them these rights, why did Congress find it necessary to pass special laws conferring them upon persons of color in the District of Columbia?

In conclusion, then, I will say, that, construe this matter which way we will—provided we are guided by the light surrounding us—we are forced to the conclusion that the Plaintiff in Error here, does not, by law, possess the rights claimed for him. His race has been gradual in their acquirement of the rights they now possess. They first got freedom—citizenship; and second, the right to vote; and when they show me, in the statute book, an enactment giving them the right to hold office, I will cheerfully submit. At present, however, they have no such right in Georgia.

————

ATLANTA, GEORGIA, June 11, 1869.

The Court opened at 10 o'clock—His Honor the Chief Justice presiding.

ARGUMENT OF GOVERNOR JOHNSON.

EX-GOVERNOR JAMES JOHNSON, of Counsel for Plaintiff in Error, said:

MAY THE COURT PLEASE:

As I shall have occasion to analyze some of the rulings of the Judge below presiding in this case, I deem it proper to say here that I believe him to be a gentleman in his bearing, and that the rulings made by him in this case were made upon conviction of their correctness. What I have to say therefore, in reference to them, is not intended in any way to reflect upon him, individually; but to expose the legal errors he may have commited.

I call your Honors' attention first to the record in this case. By the action of the presiding Judge, the Plaintiff in Error had not only the misfortune to have this case decided adversely to him, but, after the decision was rendered, by the further action of that officer an additional labor was illegally imposed upon him. The Supreme Court of the United States never suffers an appropriate occasion to pass without putting their censure upon the conduct of parties in Courts below in unnecessarily swelling the record presented to them. The law of this State provides that when exception shall be taken in the course of proceedings below, it shall be the duty of the presiding Judge to certify to the objected points ; and to certify, in that connection, only so much of the testimony as is material to a clear understanding of the case. That is reasonable and proper, and it is the law.

The Judge in this case required that his argument, in pronouncing his judgment, should be made part and parcel of the Bill of Exceptions. It was not material to a clear understanding of the case, and the reason given for it was that he had ordered it on the minutes, and that it thereby became a part of the record. If that were so, that was the very reason why it should not go into the Bill of Exceptions, for, the only legitimate office of a Bill of Exceptions is to make that appear of record which would otherwise not be of record.

Here is the argument of the Judge, incorporated by his requirement, into this Bill of Exceptions ; here is a policy of insurance—the whole of it, required to be put into this Bill of Exceptions. If any of it was at all relevant to the case, one line would have done. Here, also, may be found the testimony of witnesses deposing in Court, to whose testimony no objection or exception was made. Here, too, is the argument and the reasons of the Court below for its ruling, when the law is that good ruling consists alone of *facts*, and not of arguments. The question to be determined by this Court is not whether the Judge below did or did not make a fine argument. It is simply this: was the ruling correct? However fallacious the reasoning may have been, the ruling will be concurred in if it be *correct*, and however correct may have been the reasoning, the judgement will be reversed if it be *not* correct.

Here also, may it please the Court, are two Demurrers— one of which is a part of the transcript in this case. The Judge has no right to touch that transcript by arguments of his own, yet we find the Judge in this case, not only certifying the Bill of Exceptions according to law, but actually taking occasion to put under one of these Demurrers that " this Demurrer was withdrawn." If he has any fact that he wishes to make appear in reference to the proceedings, it must be incorporated in the Bill of Exceptions, and not be shown by "amendments" to the transcript after it has the seal of the Court annexed to it. When he has signed the minutes, they are beyond his reach and control, and he has no authority to touch them, any more than a private party, or one of the parties to the proceeding. I mention these points, because, though it may not be material to the adjudication of this case, it is material to the country at large, to the Bar, and to this Court, that these records shall come up here properly, and devoid of all matter except such as is material or necessary to a clear understanding of the case.

Now, I ask this Court to lay down a rule that Judges below must conform to the law, and certify a Bill of Exceptions when presented; certify to the facts, and not tell lawyers and others when they draw up a Bill of Exceptions, "Go and see your adversary and agree to it, and I will sign it." It is his duty to know the facts, and to certify to them without putting such a labor on lawyers. Besides, as a learned Judge once remarked, one's adversary is the last man that would agree with him.

The point next in order, may it please the Court, is that the motion for a continuance was overruled. I shall make no lengthy remarks on it, however; neither shall I read the evidence in the case. I do not propose, either, to say that the law which fixes the requirements necessary for a continuance, divests the Court below of all discretion. My opinion is, that it is impracticable for the Legislature to divest the Courts of some discretion in such matters. It occurs to me that the Legislature, notwithstanding they have prescribed a certain rule by the Code, still they have made it admissible on the part of Judges below to exercise a sound legal discretion in reference to a continuance.

But whether I am right or wrong on that point, I have the same remark to make about it that I made in regard to certifying the proceedings below. It is important to the country and the interests of the profession that this Court should establish a rule, and that that rule should be a rule of action. I would not, however, ask the Court for a reversal of the judgment of the Court below in this case, simply on a refusal to continue. I present it merely that the Court may, if it see fit, establish a uniform rule of action in that connection.

I am glad that my friend Hartridge has taken occasion to remark to the Court, that he holds himself bound by the record, and that nothing that may be said by individuals outside of the record can properly be considered by the Court.

This record contains two Demurrers. It shows the further fact, that on the day of trial the Defendant—the Plaintiff in

Error here—filed a plea and also a Demurrer; that that Demurrer, so filed on the day on which the plea was filed, was heard and considered by the Court, and a regular formal judgment pronounced upon it; so that the Demurrer filed at the time of trial was not withdrawn, but was heard, considered and pronounced upon.

THE CHIEF JUSTICE: Let me see if I understand your point. An exception was made by Counsel for Plaintiff in Error, not by parole, as is usual, but in writing. That was taken up and heard before the case was submitted to the jury, and a ruling had upon the law of the case. Your complaint, then, is that on the hearing of that Demurrer, you were not allowed to conclude the argument on that point?

GOV. JOHNSON: Yes, sir. I made the motion—for a Demurrer is a motion—to dismiss plaintiff's motion, because it was not according to law. It was upon the question of fact that we went to the jury.

THE CHIEF JUSTICE: I want you to agree as to the facts.

COL. HARTRIDGE: We cannot agree as to the facts, sir. We will have to leave that to be decided by the record.

THE CHIEF JUSTICE: The point I want to get at is whether the Judge pronounced a decision on the *Demurrer* before the *facts* went to the jury?

COL. HARTRIDGE: He did, sir.

GOV. JOHNSON: The facts, may it please your Honors, are not at all complicated. Clements, being a private individual, could not, without the leave of the Court, file an Information in the nature of a *Quo Warranto*, against the Defendant. At least, that we presume to have been the understanding of Counsel; and they applied to the Court for leave to use the prerogative writ; and, in their petition—which the Judge here calls an application—for leave to file this information, they stated the material facts of their case as they did in the Information itself. The defendants were notified that such a petition had been presented, and they were called upon to show cause why leave should not be granted. I was absent at the time, but before leaving I drew up a Demurrer to put in to the application for leave to file a *Quo Warranto*, and Mr. Stone presented it, showing cause.

He withdrew that Demurrer. Thereupon the Court below ordered that the Solicitor General, in the name of the State, should file an Information in the nature of a *Quo Warranto*, against the Defendant below. It was drawn up, the Defendant was served with a copy of it, and we were notified to appear at a certain day. That day arrived. Mr. Stone could not be present; but before leaving he drew up the affidavit for a continuance. Before the day of trial, I drew up an answer, denying the facts alleged in the Information, and drew a Demurrer.

On the day of trial, I filed that answer, as this Bill of Exceptions announces in terms too specific to be doubted. I filed the demurrer with it. This, therefore, is the only Demurrer that was ever filed to the Information, and it *never was withdrawn*. I insisted on being heard on it. The Bill of Exceptions will show the rest. The first Demurrer which is filed to the Petition for leave was withdrawn, leave was granted, and we are not now here taking exceptions to the Judge's order granting leave to file; but taking exceptions to his ruling, and to the manner of the trial of the Information. And, if a Demurrer was filed to the application for leave, and if, subsequently, the consent of Defendant was given that an Information might be filed, he is certainly deprived of none of his rights in pleading to the Information.

Here it is said that because this first Demurrer was withdrawn, therefore no exception could be taken to the Information itself when filed. I do not understand that to be the law. So far as my observation goes, it has been the practice in Georgia for the last thirty years that when exception is taken to a declaration or to any proceedings on the part of either the Defendant or the Plaintiff, the party excepting goes on to state the grounds of his exception, and to give his reasons therefor—quoting such authorities as bear upon the point. Then the party in opposition comes forward, and sustains his declaration or his plea, and the party taking exception is then heard in reply. In this case, however, a negro is involved, and it seems to me that when such is the case, our people too frequently lay aside their logic and their reason, and work too much from passion and prejudice. The uniform and universal rule in the argument of Exceptions and Demurrers is here set aside, for reasons injected into this Bill of Exceptions, and which I am unable to comprehend. It is important, may it please your Honors, that a point involving so much of importance to the bar and the people should be so settled here as to make it impossible for Judges below to err in dealing with it.

The next point of objection is found in the testimony of
Albert Jackson. It was sought to be proved by him that
the Defendant was *by reputation* a person of color. I objected to that testimony at the time. The Court overruled
my objection, and admitted the testimony. The gentleman
[Mr. Hartridge] says that reputation is, in certain cases, original testimony, and may be legally admitted. I admit it.
I admit that in reference to pedigree, marriage, &c., reputation as a general rule, may be received as original evidence;
but I am not prepared to say—for I believe the law to be
otherwise—that reputation is *always* admissable. As a gen
eral rule reputation as to marriage is admissable; but I apprehend that in a criminal suit, say for bigamy, the prior
marriage cannot be established by reputation. The law
says the fact must be proven by some witness cognizant of
the fact. So, too, where a question of this kind is involved
and the contest is between parties themselves as to the practice, and this question of descent comes up collaterally, then
it may be proved by reputation; then such testimony is admissable. But, where a proceeding is against an indidivid
nal, *in personam*, alleging the fact of his being of negro
descent, then the fact is not to be established by reputation,
but by proof. The authority which has been read to the
Court by the learned Counsel [Mr. Hartridge] from the
Georgia Reports was a contest where this question of descent came up between the parties as a *collateral* question
In this case, however, the entire proceeding—the head and
front of the offending—is that the Defendant below is a
person of color. That is the *only charge* against him. When
it is the main question at issue, it can certainly not be
proven by reputation.

Again, here is a physician who has studied medicine and
Ethnology, and who is called as an expert to give his opinion in this matter. I objected also to that. I did not object to his certifying to any fact within his knowledge; but
to giving his "opinion" as an "expert." I was overruled,
however, and he gave his opinion as such expert—amongst
other things stating that the weight of authority was that
the human race was not of common origin! That was a
part of his ethnological "information!" I don't think that
the law is yet disposed to give him formal rank over Moses
and the Prophets. I maintain that his opinion in that connection is worth nothing.

7

The case was then submitted to the jury. Counsel for Defendant requested the Court, in writing, to charge, as is stated in the Bill of Exceptions, that the Defendant, being in the exercise of the functions of the office, the law presumed him to have the right to exercise them, and that it was incumbent on the plaintiff to rebut that presumption by legal proof; and that if the Plaintiff failed to make out every material point in his case, they must find for the Defendent. That is the nature of the request. Such charge the Court peremptorily refused to give. The Counsel for Defendant in Error states that the manner in which it was put was calculated to mislead the jury, and therefore that the Court was right in refusing to give it. They do not assail the correctness of the request; they do not say that it was not proper and legal, but they insist that it was calculated to mislead the jury. If the request is in conformity with law, and embodies nothing but the correct principles of law applicable to that particular case, I do not understand upon what principle the Court should refuse to grant it because the jury may not understand it. The law allows no such presumption. They say, however, that the Court gave substantially the charge as requested. I must beg leave to differ with the gentlemen, for the Court, in his charge, distinctly says that the presumption sought to be drawn from it in law was not the true one, but that there was another to be drawn from it. Furthermore, he divides it into two points. I presented it as a whole. Now, when Counsel requests, what is the duty of the Court? If there is anything defective in the request, he may refuse to grant it. The Counsel must present it to him at his peril. He must see to it that there is no error in it, or, if there be, to put it in as a whole. I did so in this case. The Judge says it is not correct in law. The gentlemen here do not assail it for its incorrectness; and I hold it to be a principle of law regulating the practice in such cases, that whenever an Attorney presents a request to a Court and that request is law, the Court must give it in the language in which it is expressed. If the Court is apprehensive that the jury or the Counsel on the other side will not understand it, the Counsel or the jury have a right to ask the Court to explain it to them. The Court in this case did not ask that an explanation of this request should be made to the jury, so that they may not be misled by it. If any apprehension existed about it, the learned Counsel ought to have made the request. These points that I have presented, although they may be considered preliminary and inferior, yet are of much practical interest.

But the great question involved in this case is one of magnitude and importance far above those enumerated. That question is: Can a negro hold office in Georgia? And in the discussion of this grave question we find ourselves surrounded by the prejudices and passions of our people, and find these prejudices and passions arrayed against us—prejudices naturally growing out of differences of race, and engendered by continued strife. I hold that the people of my race should rise higher than these prejudices and give an impartial judgment on a question of this kind, according to the law and the facts, and a judgment that shall bear the scrutiny of all future time.

I consider this question to be narrowed by the Constitution and laws of this State into very narrow limits. The Constitution of the State declares that all persons born in this State shall be citizens. Whatever difference of opinion may exist as to what the term citizen may include, all agree that as used in that Constitution, negroes are citizens. What is the meaning of this word citizen? Why, in Kentucky it may mean one thing and in Pennsylvania another, according to local law. But, standing here where it does, the term "citizen" is to be understood and interpreted in its ordinary acceptation, if that can be arrived at. Gentlemen seem to disagree as to what it embraces. How is its proper meaning to be arrived at? By looking at the term itself, and at the subject matter with reference to which it was used.

When the Convention adopted the laws to which I refer, it had before it the Code of Georgia, which had been already adopted. They re-adopted it. When so re-adopting it, they found it to contain in many places the words "citizen" and "citizens." When, therefore, they placed these words in the Constitution, they placed them there with a full knowledge of the meaning of these terms in the Code, and they undoubtedly meant them to agree in meaning in both documents. They could not have intended that they should mean one thing in the Code and another and a different thing in the Constitution. The Code clearly states in express terms that among the rights of citizens shall be "*the right to hold office.*" The word "citizen," then, meaning, as it must, the same thing in both documents, the conclusion is inevitable that the negroes are entitled to hold office. A number of quotations have been read by Counsel for Defendant in Error, to show you that the provisions of the

Code and of the Constitution must be made, if possible, to stand together. Why, they clearly and plainly stand together. The Constitution says the negro is a citizen; the Code says a citizen can hold office, therefore, a negro has the right to hold office if he be legally elected or appointed thereto. The word "Senator" and the word "Representative" has each the same meaning in the Constitution that it has in the Code, and in both cases the ordinary meaning attached to them. They do not refer to women or children, although the Code says that Senators and Representatives shall be "citizens." "Male persons" only can hold these offices. A negro is a male person, and a citizen; hence he has a clear right to hold these offices, if he possesses the other necessary qualifications laid down. The Judge below calls this "strange logic!" It may look strange, but it seems to me that any other interpretation would be very strange indeed.

What was the object intended to be accomplished in the formation of this Constitution? To arrive at a just idea of its object, we must glance a little at the events of the past.

The question of slavery, having agitated the public mind of the country for years, culminated in a sectional war. As the armies of the Federal Government advanced Southward and took possession of the insurgent States, at each and every point of which, as they took possession, the shackles fell from the limbs of the slaves. The proclamation of the President declaring these people free, followed in the wake of the soldiery; and the fact accomplished by power, was then made law. The old-time slave was then a freeman, not merely in point of fact, but in law also. All men were henceforth free in Georgia: no slave stood upon her soil. But Georgia stood without a State Government—the Government established by the Confederacy having been overthrown by the armies of the Union. In this emergency, certain Acts, called Reconstruction Acts, were passed. They, among other things, authorized the assembling of a Convention in this State to provide a Constitution therefor; and they authorized the registration of people to vote for members of that convention. These measures *required* the Convention to take a certain position on the question of slavery. The object of the Government—the legislative authority—was to put such expressions in this Constitution as should forever abolish all legal and political distinctions on account of race or color. Its object was to destroy forever the distinctions growing out of the peculiar institutions of slavery;

and to enable all men to stand upon a basis of equality before the law.

That Convention assembled, having in view the object of conforming to these requirements. When it had completed its labors, believing that it had conformed to all the requirements of Congress, and that it had provided effectually that there should be no distinction in regard to suffrage or officeholding, on account of race or color, the Constitution was adopted. The people subsequently ratified it at the polls with that understanding, and it was submitted to Congress for approval. Congress approved it with that understanding—ordering, however, that certain portions of it not pertinent to this issue, should be expunged.

The Convention which framed that Constitution had for a portion of its *personnel* a number of enfranchised negroes. The Legislature elected under the new Constitution had in it also a number of emancipated slaves. The General in command refused to recognize that Legislature as a body until it should purge itself of all ineligible members. It then made a pretended purgation; and not one word was raised at that time, in reference to the eligibility of black men. They sat in each House as eligible members, and acted and voted as such. It is, therefore, too late now for gentlemen to cry out that this idea of negro office-holding is a *new* idea. In that regard they are estopped by the action to which I have referred. The General Government, too—both the Executive and Legislative branches of it—have recognized the right of the black man to hold office.

Several arguments *ab inconvenienti* have been made to the Court, to which I do not think it necessary to reply.

It is complained, however, by one of the Counsel that it could certainly not have been the intention of the Convention or the Government, on account of the previous condition of these people and their present ignorance, to abolish these distinctions, as to office, which the old-time policy would seem to justify. But, may it please the Court, the wise, the crafty, and the rich of this world, need no political power. The ignorant, the simple and the poor are those who need the protection of the law. This world was not made for Cæsar only: it was made for humanity. And as the ignorant and the poor who are struggling for subsistance form nine-tenths of that humanity, it is necessary that some means should be placed at their disposal by which they can protect themselves against oppression and wrong.

Will gentlemen tell me what is to be done with these

poor people—without homes, without houses, without land, occupation or money? Is it not at the very least the duty of the Government to see that they are protected in their personal rights?—to see that they are not oppressed? And should this protection be afforded by military power rather than the more peaceful, but not less powerful, measure of placing in their hands a ballot and giving them the right to aspire, with the white race, to such offices as they can fill? But, it is said "we of the white race are superior," and so we are. We are superior in education, superior in science, superior in resources, and superior in civilization. They are wanting in these, and such being the case, for my own part, I have no apprehension that in a contest for superiority they would ever outstrip us. I fear not "negro domination." They are far behind us, and we could well afford to give them opportunity. Besides, we are thirty millions while they are but four millions. Our race will naturally increase, and, by immigration, will rapidly outstrip theirs, and soon destroy even the present ratio of numbers. There is, therefore, no need to fear that we shall ever become a negro government.

This is a white man's Government and it will continue so to be. And I want my race to be so far superior in the sublime attributes of generosity, morality, and understanding, that however inferior, ignorant, or oppressed a human being may be, they will concede it to be their duty to extend to him a full and liberal measure of justice, generous kindness and liberality. By these means the white race will not be degraded, but rather *elevated* to a degree still higher in the scale of civilization. It will be made more grand, more noble, more aspiring, than before. There is and can be no danger of humiliation from the emancipation of slaves. And I trust the day is not far distant when admiration or love for slavery will be extinguished in each and every bosom in the land; and when every Southern heart will rejoice that, by the exigencies of war, and in the providence of God, these unfortunate people were emancipated, even against the will of both the belligerents. And I trust that they will further rejoice in the confident belief that this great land of ours shall be one of freedom for all peoples and all races and all tongues—shall be a land of Universal Freedom now and through all succeeding generations.

[NOTE:
By the Revised Code of Georgia, the Judges of the Supreme Court are required, in open Court, to read the "Decision" of the Court—that is, the principles on which the judgment is based. This "Decision" forms the head notes of the "Opinion" which is afterwards written, sustaining by argument and authority the decision thus rendered.—E. D.]

SUPREME COURT CHAMBERS,   }
ATLANTA, GEORGIA, June 15, 1869. }

The Court opened at 10 o'clock, A. M.—His Honor, the Chief Justice, presiding.

THE CASE STATED.

Before announcing the judgment of the Court, in the case of Richard W. White, Clerk of the Superior Court of Chatham county, Plaintiff in Error, *vs.* The State of Georgia, *ex relatione* Wm. J. Clements, Defendant in Error, Judge McCay said :

The case of Richard W. White, Plaintiff in Error, against the State of Georgia on the relation of Wm. J. Clements, Defendant in Error, comes before this Court on the following state of facts :

Wm. J. Clements applied to the Judge of the Superior Court of Chatham county, alleging that at an election which had been held in that county for a Clerk of the Superior Court, he and Richard W. White were the sole candidates. That Richard W. White had got a majority of the votes, but that he, Clements, had also got a good many votes, and that no other persons were running. The petition further stated that Richard W. White had been declared elected, and had been commissioned, and was in the actual performance of the duties of the office, and that Richard W. White was a person of color, having one-eighth or more of African blood in his veins. That, therefore, under the laws of Georgia, he was ineligible to office, and further, that under the laws of Georgia, as White, the person having received the majority of votes, was ineligible, he, Clements, having received the next highest number of votes, was entitled to the position. He prayed the Court for leave to file an Information for a *Quo Warranto*. To that petition, of which White was notified, he, White, filed a Demurrer. Subsequently, however, he withdrew the Demurrer to that Petition, and the Information issued in the name of the State of Georgia. The Court passed an order directing the Solicitor General for that Circuit to make out an Information in the name of the State, reciting, in effect, the facts which had been recited in Clements' Petition, and calling upon White to show cause why a *Judgment Absolute* should not issue against him, depriving him of the office and putting Clements in. White, at the proper time fixed by the Information for answering, filed a Demurrer to the Information, and at the same time filed an Answer, denying that he was a person of color, or that he had one-eighth or more of African blood in his veins.

On this the Court summoned a jury for the purpose of trying the issue. When the jury had been sworn, the Defendant below—the Plaintiff here—called up his Demurrer to the Information. It is stated in the record that the Plaintiff in the Information had no objection to taking up the Demurrer at that time, but consented; and the Court heard the motion as an independent motion before the case was submitted to the jury. The Court decided that in the argument on that motion—that Demurrer—Clements, the movant in the general proceeding, was entitled to open and conclude the argument—that the matter being before the jury, the general rule which gives to the party moving in a Demurrer the right to open and conclude did not apply.

The Court heard the argument on the Demurrer and overruled the Demurrer. The case then went to the jury on the issue of fact whether or not White had one-eighth or more of African blood in his veins. On the trial there were various questions made as to the testimony. One witness testified that the Defendant, White, was reputed in the neighborhood to be a colored person. Another witness testified that he (the witness) was a registrar of voters; that when White registered, he, the registrar, had affixed opposite White's name the letter "C," to denote that he was a person of color; that he subsequently posted the lists in a public place, and that they had remained there two or three weeks without any application having been made to him to have that letter "C" erased or changed. It did not appear, however, that there was any notice to White that this letter "C" had been placed opposite to his name, nor did it appear that it was the law or the practice that if he had applied to have it corrected, that they would have corrected it; in other words, that it was the part or the duty of the officer at all to make that entry. At least, it has not so been made to appear to us.

This evidence was objected to by the defense but admitted by the Court. The Court also admitted as evidence the statement by a physician, an examining physician of an insurance company, that at a previous time he had examined White, and had pronounced him a mulatto. There was no testimony by the physician of what his opinion was at the time of the trial. The testimony was that at some previous time he had examined him, and was, at that previous time, of opinion that he was a mulatto.

In the further progress of the trial they proposed to introduce a copy of an application for a life insurance on the life of White in favor of his wife, which application purported to be signed by White. The application does not seem to have had a word in it as to whether White was a white man or a black man; it gave no indication as to his color: but on the *back* of it there was an entry by a person who purported to be an examining physician, that White was a mulatto. The witness swore at first that he thought White signed the paper, but swore afterwards that he didn't know whether White had signed it or whether his wife had signed it for him. Objection was made to this paper on three grounds: one, that it was a copy-paper, though it was proven that the original was in New York; another, that there was no proof that the original had been executed; and third, that in any event the paper amounted to nothing.

Another witness, also a physician, swore that he was a practicing physician, and that he had studied the science of ethnology; that that science taught men the rules by which the race of man was ascertained; and this witness gave his opinion upon the point. The Court admitted his opinion, that White was a person of color, as being the opinion of an expert. The case went to the jury on this testimony. There were some objections to the charge of the Court which we, however, have not noticed, because we didn't think the point very material. The jury found for the Plaintiff in the Information. Thereupon the Court passed judgment, deposing White from his position as Clerk of the Superior Court, and declaring that Clements was entitled to hold that office.

This case has been argued before us with a great deal of learning and ability.

This Court has agreed upon the judgment it will deliver in this case, but not upon the reasons upon which this judgment is founded. The Court all agree that the judgment in the Court below ought to be reversed—this Court being unanimously of opinion that the Court below erred in various of its rulings on the trial, and on the question of the argument on the Demurrer.

A majority of the Court, the Chief Justice and myself, agree in the judgment that the Court below erred in overruling the Demurrer, it being our opinion that under the Code of Georgia a person of color is eligible to office in Georgia. My brother Brown, however, and myself do not exactly agree upon the grounds upon which we base that judgment. The statutes of the State of Georgia require that the Court shall agree in the *decision* which it makes—the principle upon which it puts the case which it decides; and as my brother Warner, whilst he agrees to the general judgment, puts his opinion upon one set of grounds, and my brother, the Chief Justice, puts his upon another, while I put mine upon a third, we are unable to agree upon a statement of the general principles upon which we put our judgment. Hence, under the statute, we shall each give a statement of the ground upon which we assent to the judgment of this Court.

I will, therefore, now read the grounds upon which the whole Court bases its decision; the ground upon which the majority of the Court bases its decision; and I shall also announce the principles upon which I, myself, hold that the Court below erred.

As this is a case of a good deal of public importance, involving not only the rights of the Defendant, and this Plaintiff in Error, but of a very large portion of the people of this State, and one in whom there is a great deal of interest taken, I have reduced to writing, in detail, the principles of my decision; and I will preface the reading of the judgment of the whole Court and of the majority of the Court, with some written remarks—preferring to do that rather than make a parole introduction.

REMARKS OF JUDGE McCAY.

Whatever may have been, under the Constitution of the United States, the abstract truth as to the political condition and status of the people of Georgia at the close of the late war, from the stand-point of a mere observer, it seems to me perfectly conclusive that the several branches of the present State Government are shut up to the doctrine that the Constitution and frame of civil Government in existence in this State on the 1st of January, 1861, with all its disabilities and restrictions, was totally submerged in the great revolution which, from 1861 to 1865, swept over the State. Early in June, 1865, the Governor of 1860 was in prison at Washington, and there was not, in the whole State, a single civil officer in the exercise of the functions of his office.

The whole body lately acting had been chosen under the laws of the Confederate States, and the incumbents of 1860 had all either died or resigned or renounced their positions as officers under the Constitution of the United States, by swearing fealty to the Confederacy and repudiating the government of the Union.

The people of the State were, in the language of the President, without civil government of any kind—in anarchy. The State, as a State of the Federal Union, still existed, but without any frame of civil government regulating, restraining and directing the exercise of its functions. From that time until the present State Government went into operation, the government of the State was with more or less completeness in the hands of the military authorities of the United States, and the entire ancient civil polity of the State, was totally ignored. Directly in the teeth of the old Constitution, the people of color were recognized as freemen, and as entitled to equal, legal, and political rights, with the whites. The Convention of 1867 met under the laws of the United States, and was elected and composed in total disregard of all the provisions and presumptions, qualifications, disqualifications, and distinctions of the old organization.

The black people participated in its election, and in its composition, on equal terms, in theory at least, with the white, and nothing can to my mind be plainer that that by the whole theory then acted upon, then were recognized as forming an integral part of the sovereign people then assembled in convention to form for their common benefit a constitution and frame of civil government.

Such being the facts of the case, it appears to me that this Court, deriving its whole authority from the Constitution then framed, and sworn to support it, is, from the very nature of the case, absolutely prohibited from recognizing as then or now, in force, either the Constitution of 1860 or 1865, or any of the legal or political disabilities or distinctions among the people, dependent upon them or either of them.

The Convention met under the laws of the United States, to form a Constitution for a people without civil Government.

It had nothing to repeal, nothing to modify, nothing to grant. None of the old Constitutions of the State were in operation—the Convention met under entirely new ideas and new presumptions. It represented a new people—a people among whom slavery had ceased, and among whom black people as well as white were recognized as forming part of the political society, and entitled to equal participation in its rights, privileges and immunities.

It is not necessary, for the purposes of this argument, that this theory shall be proven to have been a legal one under the Constitution of the United States. It is sufficient to state that it is true as a fact, and that the present State Government is based upon it.

If, when the Convention met in December, 1867, the ancient Constitution of the State, or any of its legal or political disabilities or disqualifying distinctions upon persons of color were of force, then the Convention was itself illegal; the present State Government is illegal, this Court is illegal. His Honor, the Chief Justice, has his proper place in the Executive Chair, my respected associate and myself are private citizens, the Plaintiff in Error is a slave, and the whole political history of the State since the imprisonment of Governor Brown, in June, 1855, a gigantic illegality.

I am aware that a very large class of our most intelligent people, so, at this moment, honestly believe: to them this argument is not directed; but it seems to me, that to a Judge holding his office under the present State Government, forming an essential part of its machinery, these views must be of overwhelming force. If he assumes the power to decide at all, he must, it seems to me, base his judgment upon principles which do not, if adopted in his own case, utterly subvert his own authority.

I make these remarks with the greatest deference to the integrity and to the sound legal acumen of my associates. Honest men see things in different lights, and it is as presumptious as it is uncharitable, for one man to set up his convictions as the necessary guide of the conscience of another. These are my convictions, and as a matter of course, I must act upon them, and accordingly, under the rules prescribed by the statute, I announce, as the general principles, controling my judgment in this case, the following:

DECISION OF COURT.

By the whole Court,

First, The statement of a registrar of voters that he had marked a registered person's name with a "C" to denote that he was colored, and had posted his lists for some time in a public place, and that no application had been made to have the said "C" erased, is no evidence that the person is a colored person, it not being shown that the person knew of the entry, and that it was the subject of correction.

Second, Although a copy of a paper proven to be beyond the jurisdiction of the Court is good secondary evidence of its contents, yet it must be shown that the original was duly executed.

Third, An application for a life insurance, though signed by the applicant, upon the back of which was an entry by the examining physician that the applicant was a mulatto, is no evidence unless it be proven that the person signed the paper after the entry on it was made by the physician and with knowledge of the entry and with intent to adopt it, or that he used the paper after the entry was made with a knowledge that such entry was there.

Fourth, The statement by an examining physician, that he had at a certain time examined a person and had then been of the opinion that the person was a mulatto, is not evidence. If the physician is an expert he must give his present opinion, and if not he must state the facts upon which he bases his opinion. Whether or not one is a person of color, that is, has African blood in his veins, is matter of opinion, and a witness may give his opinion if he states the facts upon which it is based. But whether the fact that he has one-eighth or more of such blood, be matter of opinion or not—Query?

Fifth, One who testifies that he has studied the science of ethnology may give his opinion as an expert on the question of race. Its weight is for the jury.

Pedigree, relationship and race may be proven by evidence of reputation among those who know the person whose pedigree or race is in question.

The whole Court agree upon the propositions above given.

The majority of the Court agree upon this proposition. Where a *quo warranto* was issued charging that a person holding an office was ineligible, when chosen, because of his having in his veins one-eighth or more of African blood, and there was a Demurrer to the information as well as an answer denying the fact, upon which denial there was an issue and a trial before the jury: Held that by the Code of Georgia, a person having one-eighth or more of African blood in his veins is not ineligible to office in this State, and it was error in the Court to overrule the Demurrer and to charge the jury that if the Plaintiff proved the Defendant to have one-eighth or more of African blood he was ineligible to office in this State.

Whilst I agree that the Code of Georgia—the law of Georgia, as separate from the Constitution— does make persons of color eligible to office, my opinion is that eligibility is guaranteed by the Constitution of the State, and I announce these propositions as the general principles upon which my opinion is based.

1st. The Constitution of Georgia known as the Constitution of 1868, is a new Constitution, made by, and formed for, a people who at the time were, by the facts of the case, and the laws of the United States, without any legal civil Government; and as the people of Georgia, without regard to past political distinctions, and without regard to distinctions of color, participated on equal terms in the election for the Convention, and in its composition and deliberations, as well as in the final ratification of the Constitution it framed —in the construction of the Constitution, and in the investigation of what rights it guarantees, or denies, such distinctions are equally to be ignored.

2d. The rights of the people of this State, white and black, are not granted to them by the Constitution thereof. The object and effect of that instrument is not to give, but to restrain, deny, regulate, and guarantee rights; and all persons recognized by that Constitutson as citizens of the State have equal legal and political rights, except as otherwise expressly declared.

3d. It is the settled and uniform sense of the word "citizen," when used in reference to the citizens of the separate States of the United States, and to their rights as such citizens, that it describes a person entitled to every right, legal and political, enjoyed by any person in that State, unless there be some express exception, made by positive law, covering the particular person, or class of persons, whose rights are in question.

4th. Words used in a statute, or Constitution, have their ordinary signification, unless they be words of art, when they have the sense placed upon them by those skilled in the art, or unless their meaning be defined and fixed by law —in which latter case the legal meaning must prevail.

5th. By the 1648th and 1649th Sections of Irwin's Revised Code, it is expressly declared, that among the rights of citizens is the right to hold office, and that all citizens are entitled to exercise all their rights as such, unless expressly prohibited by law; and as the Constitution of 1868 expressly adopts said Code as the law of the State, when that Constitution uses the word "citizen," it uses it in the sense put upon it by the express definition of the Code it adopted.

6th. Article 1st and section 2d of the Constitution of 1868 expressly declares that all persons born in the United States, or naturalized therein, resident in this State, are citizens of this State; and as the Code adopted by the Convention in express terms declares that among the rights of citizens is the right to hold office, a colored person born in the United States, and resident in this State, is, by that section of the Constitution guaranteed eligibility to office, except when otherwise prohibited.

7th. Nor would the repeal of those sections of the Code, or their alteration, deprive a colored person of the right thus guaranteed. Since it is a settled rule that it is not in the power of the Legislature to divest a right or change a constitutional guarantee by altering the legal meaning of the word by which that guarantee was made.

8th. The right to vote involves the right to be voted for, unless otherwise expressly provided, since it is not to be presumed, without an express enactment, that the principal is of less dignity or rights than the agent.

9th. There being in the Constitution of 1868 various special disqualifications of electors for particular offices, and four separate sections detailing disqualifications for *any* office, and a black skin not being mentioned as one of these disqualifications, under the rule that the expression, &c., of one thing is the exclusion of others, persons of color, electors, are not disqualified from holding office.

10th. There never has been in this State, at any period of its history, any denial in terms of the right to vote or to hold office to colored persons, as such. By the old law, they were either slaves or free persons of color, and these rights were denied them by declaring that they were not, and could not be, citizens of the State; and when Article 1, Section 2 of the Constitution of 1868 recognized them as citizens, the right to vote and to hold office, except as otherwise provided by the Constitution, was, *ex vi termini*, also guaranteed to them.

11th. Ineligibility to office involves not only the denial to the person claiming the place the right to be chosen, but, what is of far greater moment, the right of the selecting power to choose; and to make out a case of ineligibility there must be such a state of affairs as establishes not only the want of power to be chosen, but a denial of power in the selecting party to choose.

12th. The people of a State, in their collective capacity, have every right a political society can have except such as they have conferred upon the United States, or on some department of the State Government, or have expressly denied to themselves by their Constitution; and as the right to select a public officer is a political right, the people, or that branch of the Government clothed by the Constitution with the power to choose, may select whomsoever it will, unless the right to choose a particular person, or class of persons, is expressly taken away by the Constitution.

OPINION OF CHIEF JUSTICE BROWN.

Chief Justice Brown then read from his written opinion, as follows:

The view which I take of the rights of the parties litigant in this case, under the Code of Georgia, renders it unnecessary for me to enter into an investigation of the question; whether the Fourteenth Amendment of the Constitution of the United States, or the Second Section of the First Article of the Constitution of Georgia, which in substance is identical with the Fourteenth Amendment, confers upon colored citizens the right to hold office. If the respondent in this case acquires the right by grant found in either of the said Constitutions, or in the Code of this State, it is sufficient for all the purposes of the case at bar, and entitles him to a reversal of the judgment of the Court below, which was adverse to his right.

The third paragraph of the Ninth Article of the Constitution of this State adopts, in subordination to the Constitution of the United States, and the laws and treaties made in pursuance thereof; and in subordination to the said Constitution of this State; the "body of lows known as the Code of Georgia, and the acts amendatory thereof, which" said

Code and acts are embodied in the printed book known as
Irwin's Code," "except so much of the said several Statutes,
Code and Laws, as may be inconsistent with the Supreme
law herein recognized."

The Code, Section 1646, classifies natural persons into
four classes: 1st. Citizens, 2d. Residents, 3d. Aliens, 4th.
Persons of color.

Section 46 of the Code declares that, All *white* persons
born in this State, or in any other State of the Union, who
are or may become residents of this State, with the intention of remaining herein; all *white* persons naturalized
under the laws of the United States, and who are, or may
become, residents of this State with the intention of remaining herein; all persons who have obtained a right to citizenship under former laws, and all children wherever born,
whose father was a citizen of this State at the time of the
birth of such children; or in case of posthumous children
at the time of his death, are held and deemed citizens of
this State.

By the Code the distinction is therefore clearly drawn between citizens who are *white* persons and persons of color.

In other words, none are citizens under the "printed
book known as Irwin's Code" but white persons. Having
specified the class of persons who are citizens, the Code proceeds, in Section 1648, to define some of the rights of citizens, as follows:

"Among the rights of citizens are the enjoyment of personal security, of personal liberty, private property and the
disposition thereof, the elective franchise, *the right to hold
office*, to appeal to the Courts, to testify as a witness, to perform any civil function. and to keep and bear arms."

Section 1649 declars that, "*All* citizens are entitled to
exercise *all* their rights as such unless specially prohibited
by law."

Section 1650 prohibits females from exercising the elective
franchise, or holding civil office.

Section 1651 prohibits minors from the exercise of civil
functions, till they are of legal age.

Sections 1652 and 1653 prohibit certain criminals, and
persons *non compos mentis*, from exercising certain rights of
citizens.

Article 3, Chapter 1, Title 1, Part 2, of the Code defines
the rights of the Fourth class of natural persons, desig-
nated as persons of color; giving them the right to make
contracts; sue and be sued, give evidence, inherit, purchase

8

and sell property; and to have material rights, security of personal estate, &c., embracing the usual civil rights of citizens, but does not confer citizenship. Thus the Code stood prior to its adoption by the new Constitution.

As already shown, it was adopted, in subordination to the Constitution, and must yield to the fundamental law, whenever in conflict with it. In so far as the Code had conferred rights on the colored race there is no conflict, and no repeal. The Constitution took away no rights then possessed by them under the Code, but it enlarged their rights as defined in the Code, by conferring upon them the right of citizenship. It transferred them from the fourth class of natural persons, under the above classification, who were denied citizenship by the Code, to the first class, as citizens.

The 46th Section of the Code limited citizenship to white persons. The Constitution struck out the word white, and made all persons born or naturalized in the United States, and resident in this State, citizens, without regard to race or color. It so amended Section 46 of the Code, as greatly to enlarge the class of citizens. But it repealed no part of Section 1648, which defines the rights of citizens.

It did not undertake to define the rights of a citizen. It left that to the Legislature, subject to such guarantees as are contained in the Constitution itself, which the Legislature cannot take away. It declares expressly that no law shall be made or enforced which shall " abridge the privileges or immunities of citizens of the United States, or of this State." It is not necessary to the decision of this case to inquire, what are the "privileges and immunities" of a citizen? which are guaranteed by the 14th Amendment to the Constitution of the United States, and by the Constitution of this State. Whatever they may be, they are protected against all abridgement by legislation. This is the full extent of the constitutional guarantee. All rights of the citizen, not embraced within these terms, if they do not embrace all, are subject to the control of the Legislature.

Whether the "privileges and immunities" of the citizen embrace political rights, including the right to hold office, I need not now inquire. If they do, that right is guaranteed alike by the Constitution of the United States, and the Constitution of Georgia; and is beyond the control of legislation. If not, that right is subject to the control of the Legislature as the popular voice may dictate; and in that case the Legislature would have power to grant or restrict it at pleasure, in case of white persons as well as of persons of color. The Constitution of Georgia has gone as far as

the 14th Amendment has gone, and no further. An authoritative construction of the 14th Amendment by the Supreme
Court of the United States upon this point would be equally
binding as a construction of the Constitution of the State of
Georgia, which is in the same words.

Georgia has complied fully with the terms dictated by
Congress in the formation of her Constitution. She has
stopped nothing short, and gone nothing beyond. The
highest judicial tribunal of the Union will no doubt finally
settle the meaning of the terms "privileges and immunities"
of the citizen, which legislation cannot abridge; and the
people of Georgia, as well as those of all the other States,
must conform to, and in good faith abide by, and carry out,
the decision. All the rights, of all the citizens, of every
State, which are included in the phrase " privileges and immunities " are protected against legislative abridgement by
the fundamental law of the Union. Those not so embraced,
unless included within some other constitutional guaranty
are subject to legislative action. The same rights which
the Fourteenth Amendment to the Constitution of the
United States confers upon, and guarantees to, a colored
citizen of Ohio, are conferred upon and guaranteed to every
colored citizen of Georgia, by the same amendment, and by
the Constitution of this State, made in conformity to the reconstruction acts of Congress.

Whatever may or may not be the *privileges* and *immunities* guaranteed to the colored race, by the Constitution of
the United States and of this State, it cannot be questioned
that both Constitutions make them citizens. And I think
it very clear that the Code of Georgia upon which alone I
base this opinion, which is binding upon all her inhabitants
while of force, confers upon *all* her citizens the right to hold
office, unless they are prohibited by some provision found
in the Code itself. I find no such prohibition in the Code
affecting the rights of this respondent. I am, therefore, of
the opinion that the judgment of the Court below is erroneous, and I concur in the judgment of reversal.

REMARKS BY JUDGE WARNER.

At this point, his Honor Judge Warner, before commencing to read his written opinion, opened with the following remarks. He said:

I dissent from so much of the judgment of the majority of the Court as reverses the judgment of the Court below overruling the Demurrer. The question involved in that Demurrer was, Whether a colored citizen under the Constitution and laws of this State has the legal right to hold office under her authority.

The State is the source and fountain of office; there can be no dispute about that. And when a person, whether white or colored, claims a legal right to hold an office under her authority, he must show his legal right to do so either under the Constitution or statutes of the State or the common law of the State. The difficulty in regard to colored citizens in my judgment—the legal difficulty—in their way, of holding office in this State under the existing law, consists in this:

They are a new class which has been incorporated into the body politic in this State. It is unnecessary to inquire by what means, but they have been incorporated into the body politic of the State—made a part thereof.

They cannot claim a common law right to hold office in the State, for they had not exercised that right so long that "the memory of man runneth not to the contrary." They have recently been incorporated into the body politic of the State. They cannot claim a common law right to hold office under the authority of the State. In my judgment the Constitution did not confer that right upon them, nor does the Code of Georgia confer that right upon them, for it should be remembered that the Code of Georgia was adopted by the Legislature prior to their being made citizens. Colored citizens were not in contemplation of the lawmakers when that Code was adopted. That Code was adopted as the law of the State on the 1st of January, 1863, and all the provisions that are made in that Code were made for the class of citizens which are specified and recognized in that Code as citizens. Colored citizens were not contemplated by the law makers—they were not in view at all. These provisions were not made in reference to them in any manner whatever, for they were not then citizens of the State; they were incorporated into the body politic subsequently to the Code, and when the Constitution adopted that Code it adopted it as a whole, as it stood, without making any alterations in it.

Then colored citizens cannot claim a common law right to hold office in the State: the Constitution in my judgment did not confer the right upon them to hold office, and the Code did not confer it, because that is not the expression of the legislative will of the State since they became citizens thereof, and can have no application to them. The Code, when it speaks of the rights of citizens, speaks of that class which the Code itself recognized as citizens at that time. It did not provide for any other class who might thereafter become citizens. It only provided for that class who were citizens at the time, and nobody else—that class of citizens only were in the purview of the lawmakers when they adopted it.

The colored citizens having been incorporated into the body politic subsequently to the adoption of that Code, they must either derive their right to hold office under some public law of the State, either under the Constitution of 1868 or by the common law, or by some law that has been enacted—some expression of the public will of the State—since they became citizens. That is my point.

Has there been any expressed public will of the State as to their right to hold office since they became citizens thereof? If there has, and the rights have been conferred upon them, they are entitled to exercise them. If there has not, they cannot exercise them, and it is no answer to say that because they are not prohibited from exercising office they can do so. Unless the right was conferred upon them previously they have not got it, although there may be no prohibition; for prohibition could not prohibit that which did not exist. If they have not got the right either under the Constitution or some public law of the State the fact that they are not prohibited from exercising it amounts to nothing. They must have the previous right.

The distinction between the rights of colored citizens to hold office in this State and white citizens is: The white citizen had a common law right to hold office in the State—a right that has existed so long long that "the memory of man runneth not to the contrary." There was no law in this State previous to the adoption of the Code in 1863 conferring the right upon white citizens to hold office, and that declaration in the Code is only the substance of the common law. When the Code says it should be one of the rights of citizens to hold office, it only affirmed what was the common law, and what was the usage—the substance of a custom so long that the memory of no man runs to the contrary. The white citizen, native-born and naturalized, had a common law right to hold office, because he had exercised it so long that "the memory of man runneth not to the contrary;" but the colored citizen when he was introduced into the body politic could not claim that right. We all know the time was when he did not exercise it, and therefore he cannot claim a common law right as the white citizen can.

A naturalized citizen had the common law right to be President of the United States. That was his common law right, and hence there was a prohibition put into the Constitution to prohibit a naturalized foreigner from exercising that common law right. The moment he was naturalized as a citizen he had the common law right to hold office, and in order to restrain him they put in the prohibition that nobody should be President but a native born citizen. The prohibition prohibited the exercise of his common law right, as it was thought necessary to prohibit him from its exercise.

The State being the source and fountain of office, she may grant to any class of her citizens by some public law, either common, statute or by the Constitution—it does not matter which, but the party who claim to exercise it must show the ground—the law upon which he bases that right.

As I have said, the colored citizen recently incorporated into the body politic cannot claim it under the common law right. He must derive it either from the Constitution or some statute. I say there has no statute been passed since he was made a citizen—there has been no expression of the public will of the State since he was a citizen, that it was her will and desire that he should hold office. All the declarations of the Code, all the enactments of the Code were made prior to the time when he became a citizen, he was not embraced or included therein, and not in the perview of the law-makers who made that Code, and therefore that is no expression of the public will of the State as to his right to hold office when he was not a citizen at that time. It applies exclusively to that class who are recognized as citizens.

DISSENTING OPINION OF JUDGE WARNER.

[Here the Judge, reading from his written opinion, said:]

The Defendant is a person of color, having, as the record states, one-eighth of negro or African blood in his veins, who claims to be lawfully entitled to hold and exercise the duties of the office of Clerk of the Cuperior Court. And the question presented for our consideration and judgment is: Whether a person of color of the description mentioned in the record is legally entitled to hold office in this State under the Constitution and laws thereof.

The Fourteenth Amendment to the Constitution of the United States declares that "all persons born or naturalized in the United States and subject to the jurisdiction thereof, are citizens of the United States and the State wherein they reside. No State shall make or enforce any law which shall abridge the privileges or immunities of citizens of the United States." The Constitution of this State declares that "all persons born or naturalized in the United States and resident in this State are hereby declared citizens of this State, and no law shall be made or enforced which shall abridge the privileges or immunities of citizens of the United States or of this State."

From the time of the adoption of the Fourteenth Amendment, and the adoption and ratification of the Constitution of this State in 1868, the Defendant became, notwithstanding his color and African blood, a citizen of the United States and is entitled to all the privileges and immunities of a citizen. Does the fact that the Defendant was made a citizen of the State with all the privileges and immunities of a citizen thereof confer upon him the legal right to hold office in this State as such citizen? When we take into consideration the condition and object of creating an office, and by what authority it is conferred upon a citizen, the distinction between the privileges and immunities of a citizen as such, and his right to hold office, will be at once apparent. It will be seen that the privileges and immunities of a citizen, as such is one thing, and that his legal right to hold office as such, citizen under the authority of the State is another, and quite a different question.

What is an office? "An office," says Bacon, "is a *right* to exercise a public function, or employment, and to take the fees and emoluments belonging to it. An officer is one who is *lawfully invested with an office*. It is said that the word *officium* principally implies a *duty*, and in the next place the *charge of such duty;* and that it is a rule that where one man hath to do with another's affairs against his will, and without his leave, that this is an office, and he who is in it is an officer. By the ancient common law, officers ought to be honest men, legal and sage, *et qui melius sciant et possint officis illi intendere;* and this, says my Lord Coke, was the policy of prudent antiquity, that officers did even give grace to the place, and not the *place only* to grace the officer." 7th Bacon Ab. 279—Title offices and officers. Blackstone says: "The King, in England, is the fountain of honor, and of *office,* and the reason given is that the law supposes that no one can be so good a judge of an officer's merits and services as the King who employs him-

" From the same principle also arises the prerogative of creating and disposing of offices : for honors and offices are in their nature convertible and synonymous. All officers under the Crown carry in the eye of the law an honor along with them; because they imply a superiority of parts and abilities, being supposed to be always filled with those that are most able to execute them." 1st Bl. Com. 271, 2. Offices, says Blackstone, are a right to exercise a public or private employment, and to take the fees and emoluments thereto belonging, and are also incorporeal hereditaments. 2d. Bl. Com. 36.

All citizens of the State, whether white or colored, male or female, minors or adults, idiots or lunatics, are entitled to have all the privileges and immunities of citizens, but it does not follow that all of these different classes of citizens are entitled to hold office under the public authority of the State because the privileges and immunities of citizens are secured to them. The State, in this country, as the Crown in Europe, is the fountain of honor and of office, and she who desires to employ any class of her citizens is the best judge of their fitness and qualifications therefor. An officer of the State as we have shown has to do with another's affairs " against his will and without his leave;" and such officer must have the authority of the State to perform these public duties against the will of the citizen and without his leave. This authority must be conferred upon the citizen by some public law of the State from that class of her citizens which in her judgment will best promote the general welfare of the State. The right to have and enjoy the immunities and privileges of a citizen of a State does not confer upon him the right to serve the State in any official capacity until that right is expressly granted to him by law. Mr. Justice Curtis in his dissenting opinion in the case of Dred Scott *vs.* Sanford, says "so in all the States numerous persons, though citizens, cannot vote or cannot hold office, either on account of their age or sex, or the want of the necessary qualifications." See also case of Corfield *vs.* Coryell, 4 Washington's Circuit Court Reports 380—381 to the same point.

The Defendant, therefore, cannot legally claim any right to hold office either under the Fourteenth Amendment to the Constitution of the United States or the Constitution of this State, which make him a citizen and guarantee unto him the privileges or immmunities of a citizen; for he may well have and enjoy all the privileges and immunities of a citizen in the State without holding any office or exercising any public or official duty under the authority of the State.

The privileges and immunities of a citizen of a State do not confer the legal right to hold office under the public authority of the State. Does the public law of the State recognized and adopted by the Constitution of 1868, and known as Irwin's Code, confer upon the Defendant the legal right to hold office in this State?

The Code took effect as the public law of this State on the 1st day of January, 1863. By the 46th Section thereof it is laid down that "all white persons, born in this State or in any other State of this Union, who are, or may become residents of this State with the intention of remaining herein; all white persons naturalized under the laws of the United States, and who are or may become residents of this State with the intention of remaining herein; all persons who have obtained a right to citizenship under former laws, and all children wherever born whose father was a citizen of this State at the time of the birth of such child, or in the case of *posthumus* children at the time of his death, are held and deemed citizens of this State." "Persons having one-eighth or more of negro or African blood in their veins are not white persons in the meaning of this Code." The 1646 Section declares that "natural persons are distinguished according to their rights and status into 1st. citizens; 2d. residents, not citizens; 3d. aliens; 4th. persons of color."

Section 1647 says, "the persons to whom belong the rights of citizenship, and the mode of acquiring and losing the same have been specified in a former article: (referring to Article 46, above cited,) "Among the rights of citizens are the enjoyment of personal security, personal liberty, private property and the disposition thereof, the elective franchise, the right to hold office, to appeal to the Courts, to testify as a witness, to perform any civil function and to keep and bear arms." "All citizens are entitled to exercise all their rights as such, unless specially prohibited by law." See Sections 1647—1653.

It will be remembered that at the time of the adoption of the Code in 1868, the Defendant was not a citizen of this State and was not recognized by the Code as a citizen thereof. By the 1646th Section the status of the Defendant is defined to be a person of color and not that of a citizen.

The revised Code adopted by the Constitution of 1868, includes the act of 1866, which declares that " all negroes, mulattoes, mestizoes and their descendants, having one-eighth of negro or African blood in their veins, shall be known in this State as persons of color," and specially defines their legal rights, but the right to hold office is not one of them. (Revised Code—Section 1661.)

It is true that since the adoption of the Code the Defendant has been made a citizen, but the legal rights conferred upon citizens by the Code, were conferred upon that class of persons only who are declared and recognized by the Code as citizens of the State at the time of its adoption. When the Code declares that it shall be the right of a citizen to hold office, such right is confined to that class of persons who are recognized and declared therein to be citizens of the State, and not to any other class of persons who might thereafter become citizens. So when the Code declares that all citizens are entitled to exercise all their rights as such, unless prohibited by law, it is applicable to that class of persons only who were declared to be citizens of the State at that time, and not to any other class of persons who might thereafter be made citizens of the State, such as Chinese, Africans, or persons of color. The truth is that the public will of the State has never been expressed by any legitimate enactment in favor of the right of colored citizens to hold office in this State since they became citizens thereof.

Although these several classes of persons might be made citizens of the State with the privileges and immunities of citizens, still they could not legally hold office under the authority of the State until that right shall be conferred upon them by some public law of the State subsequent to the time at which they became citizens so as to include them in its provisions. The public will of the State, as to the legal right of that class of her citizens to hold office, has never been affirmatively expressed, but on the contrary, when the proposition was distinctly made in the Convention which formed the present Constitution to confer the right upon colored citizens to hold office in this State, it was voted down by a large majority. (See Journal of the Convention, page 312.) So far as there has been any expression of the public will of the State as to the legal right of that class of citizens known as colored citizens, since they became such, to hold office in this State, it is against that right now claimed by the Defendant.

The insurmountable obstacle in the way of the Defendant claiming a legal right to hold office in this State under the provisions of the Code, is the fact that he was not a citizen of the State at the time of its adoption. The class of persons to which he belongs were not recognized by it as citizens, and therefore he is not included in any of its provisions which conferred the right to hold office upon the class of citizens specified in the Code. The Code makes no provision whatever for colored citizens to hold office in this State; all its provisions apply exclusively to white citizens, and to no other class of citizens.

The Convention which framed the present State Constitution and declared persons of color to be citizens, could have conferred the right upon them to hold office, but declined to do so by a very decided vote of that body, and went before the people claiming its ratification upon the ground that colored citizens were not entitled to hold office under it; and there can be no doubt that the people of the State voted for its ratification at the ballot box with that understanding.

But now it is contended that the Defendant, though a colored person, is made a citizen of the State and of the United States, and that no enabling act has ever been passed to allow a naturalized citizen to hold office in this State when he possessed the other requisite qualifications prescribed by law—that the Defendant having been made a citizen of the State is entitled to hold office in the same manner as a naturalized citizen could do. The reply is that naturalized citizens were white persons and as such had a common law right to hold office—a right founded upon immemorial usage and custom, which has existed so long that "the memory of man runneth not to the contrary." The 1648th Section of the Code simply affirms the common law as to the right of white citizens to hold office in this State. No such common law right however, can be claimed in this State in favor of persons of color to hold office. They have but recently become entitled to citizenship, and have never held office in this State. In 1848, in the case of Cooper and

Worsham against the Mayor and Aldermen of the city of Savannah—4th Georgia Reports, 72—it was unanimously held and decided by this Court that free persons of color were not entitled to hold any civil office in this State. The naturalized white citizen can claim the common law right to hold office in this State; the colored citizen cannot claim any such common law right for the reason that he never exercised and enjoyed it; and that constitutes the difference between the legal right of a naturalized white citizen to hold office in this State, and a person of color who has recently been made a citizen since the adoption of the Code, and who is not embraced within its provisions.

The one can claim his common law right to hold office in the State, the other cannot; and until the State shall declare by some legislative enactment that it is her will and desire that her colored citizens shall hold office under her authority, they cannot claim the legal right to do so. We must not forget that the State is the fountain and parent of office, and may confer or refuse to confer the right to hold office upon any class of her citizens as she may think proper and expedient.

When a new class of persons are introduced into the body politic of the State, and made citizens thereof, who cannot claim a common law right to hold office therein, it is incumbent on them to show affirmatively that such law has been conferred upon them by some public law of the State since they were made citizens thereof, to entitle them to have and enjoy such right. In other words, they must show the public law of the State, enacted since they became citizens thereof, which confers the legal right claimed, before they can demand a judgment of the Court in favor of such legal right.

All male white citizens of the State, whether native born or naturalized citizens, having the necessary legal qualifications, have a common law right to hold office in this State, and, in order to deprive them of their common law right, a prohibitory statute is necessary. A naturalized citizen had a common law right to hold the office of President of the United States. Hence the prohibition in the Constitution of the United States. But, as colored citizens of the State, who have recently been made such, cannot claim a common law right to hold office in the State, no prohibitory statute is necessary to deprive them of a right which they never had under the common law or statute laws of the State. When, therefore, it is said that colored citizens have the right to hold office in the State, unless specially prohibited by law, it must be shown affirmatively that they had previously enjoyed that right. If they cannot show their right to hold office in the State, either under the common law, the Constitution, or statutes of the State, the fact that they are not specially prohibited from exercising a right which they never had, amounts to nothing so far as investing them with the right to hold office is concerned.

When and where, and by what public law of the State was the legal right to hold office therein conferred on the colored citizens thereof? If this question cannot be answered in the affirmative, and the legal authorities under which the right is claimed cannot be shown, then the argument that inasmuch as there is no special prohibition in the law against the right of colored citizens to hold office, falls to the ground. If there was no existing legal right to hold office to be prohibited, the fact that there is no prohibition does not confer such legal right. There was no legal necessity to prohibit that which did not exist.

It is not the business or the duty of courts to make the law but simply to expound and enforce existing laws which have been prescribed by the supreme power of the State.

After the most careful examination of this question I am clearly of opinion that there is no existing law of this State which confers the right upon the colored citizens thereof to hold office therein, and consequently that the Defendant has no legal right to hold or exercise the duties of the office which he claims under her authority, and that the judgment of the Court below overruling the Demurrer should be confirmed.

APPENDIX,

CONTAINING THE MESSAGES OF

HIS EXCELLENCY,

RUFUS B. BULLOCK,

GOVERNOR OF GEORGIA,

To the Legislature of that State on the Occasion of the Expulsion
of the Colored Members:

ALSO,

*The Opinions of Distinguished Legal Gentlemen of Georgia, upon
the Decision of the Supreme Court Declaring
Negroes Eligible to Office.*

APPENDIX.

In order that the history of the question of the eligibility of colored citizens to office in Georgia may be complete, the argument of His Excellency Governor Bullock, presented in Messages to the House and Senate previous to the expulsion of the colored members, is here reprinted; as also the Message of His Excellency the Governor returning to the House the joint resolution referred to in the appended opinions of legal gentlemen. It is a notorious fact that a resolution pledging the Senate to abide by the decision of the Supreme Court was *voted down* by that body, on the 8th of February, 1869, by a vote of 12 to 20, and that the House refused to entertain a similar resolution. Hence there is no foundation for the charge that the Governor vetoed a resolution pledging the Legislature to abide by the decision of the Court.

9

MESSAGE

HOUSE OF REPRESENTATIVES.

— ◆ ◆ —

EXECUTIVE DEPARTMENT, }
ATLANTA, GEORGIA, September 9, 1868. }

To the House of Representatives:

Your committee to whom was referred the subject of the
" election and eligibility of persons claiming seats" in your
body, in the place of the twenty-five members by you declared ineligible upon account of color, called upon me and
presented me with a report of the action of your body on
the subject of such alleged ineligibility; setting forth that
certain "free persons of color," therein named, from the
counties mentioned, "are, under the Constitution of the
State of Georgia, ineligible to seats on the floor" of your
House, and further appointing a committee "to whom shall
be referred the election and eligibility of persons claiming
seats from the aforesaid counties." This report is as follows:

" WHEREAS, Abram Smith, of the county of Muscogee,
has been declared ineligible to a seat on this floor; and
whereas, Thomas W. Grimes, Jr., of said county, received
the next highest number of votes cast in said county at the
late election for Representatives in the General Assembly
of this State, be it,

" *Resolved,* That the said Thomas W. Grimes, Jr., be declared a member of this body, and that the proper officer
proceed immediately to swear him in.

McDOUGALD, of Chattahoochee.

" The above resolution was amended by Mr. Tumlin, of Randolph, as follows:

1. WHEREAS, T. M. Allen, of Jasper county;
2. E. Barnes, of Hancock county;
3. T. G. Campbell, of McIntosh county;
4. G. H. Clower, of Monroe county;
5. A. Colby, of Greene county;
6. J. T. Costin, of Talbot county;
7. Monday Floyd, of Warren county;
8. S. Gardner, of Warren county;
9. W. A. Golden, of Liberty county;
10. W. H. Harrison, of Hancock county;
11. U. L. Houston, of Bryan county;
12. Philip Joiner, of Dougherty county;
13. George Linder, of Laurens county;
14. R. Lumpkin, of Macon county;
15. Romulus Moore, of Columbia county;
16. Peter O'Neal, of Baldwin county;
17. James Porter, of Chatham county;
18. A. Richardson, of Clarke county;
19. J. M. Simms, of Chatham county;
20. Abram Smith, of Muscogee county;
21. Alexander Stone, of Jefferson county;
22. H. M. Turner, of Bibb county;
23. J. Warren, of Burke county;
24. Samuel Williams, of Harris county;
25. M. Claiborne, of Burke county;

free persons of color, heretofore occupying seats on the floor of this House, are, under the Constitution of the State of Georgia, ineligible to seats on the floor of this House; and whereas, they have been so declared by said House; be it therefore.

" *Resolved,* That the persons in each of the counties aforesaid having the next highest number of votes, who are free from Constitutional ineligibility, are declared eligible and entitled to seats on the floor of this House.

"TUMLIN, of Randolph.

"On motion, a committee of three was appointed, to whom shall be referred the election and eligibility of persons claiming seats from the aforesaid counties.

"The Chair appointed the following as the committee authorized as above:

Messrs. Drake, of Upson; Lee, of Newton; Bethune, of Talbot.

"I certify the above to be a correct list of the committee appointed by the Chair, to whom shall be referred the matter above recited.

(Signed) "M. A. HARDIN,
"Clerk House of Representatives.
"ATLANTA, GA., September 4, 1868."

Your committee requested of me the names of the parties who, in the respective counties named, received the number of votes next highest to the persons so declared ineligible.

I immediately caused the necessary examination of the election returns to be made by two competent persons, sworn to the due and faithful performance of that duty, and herewith submit the names of the parties ascertained to have received in the respective counties named, the next highest number of votes, namely:

Samuel McComb, of the county of Baldwin, vice Peter McNeal;

O. G. Sparks, of the county of Bibb, vice H. M. Turner;

W. W. Greiger, of the county of Bryan, vice G. L. Houston;

J. S. Byne, of the county of Burke, vice M. Claiborne:

T. J. Burton, of the county of Burke, vice John Warren;

J. R. Saussy, of the county of Chatham, vice James Porter;

J. J. Kelley, of the county of Chatham, vice J. M. Simms;

J. H. Scott, of the county of Columbia, vice R. Moore;

Henry Morgan, of the county of Dougherty, vice Philip Joiner;

J. B. Park, of the county of Greene, vice Abraham Colby;

T. F. Brewster, of the county of Harris, vice S. Williams;

S. E. Pearson, of the county of Hancock, vice W. H. Harrison;

G. C. Carpenter, of the county of Hancock, vice E. Barnes;

Eli S. Glover, of the county of Jasper, vice F. M. Allen;

James Stapleton, of the county of Jefferson, vice A. Stone;

E. D. Barrett, of the county of Laurens, vice George Linder;

B. H. Zellner, of the county of Monroe, vice G. W. Clower;

W. L. Hitchcock, of the county of Morgan, vice Monday Floyd;

Thomas W. Grimes, of the county of Muscogee, vice Abram Smith;

J. R. Kinbrough, of the county of Talbot, vice J. T. Costin;

T. S. Hindly, of the county of Warren, vice S. Gardner.

Of the counties of Clarke, Liberty, Macon and McIntosh, the returns being incomplete, the committee are unable to report at present.

While thus participating in your action by complying with the request of your committee, I deem it to be my duty to say, that when inaugurated as Governor of this State, in presence of the General Assembly, I took a solemn oath that, to the best of my ability, I would *preserve*, *protect* and *defend* the Constitution, and though I am only able on this occasion to *defend* the Constitution by expressing a respectful objection to the action already taken, as well as that about to be taken, by the House of Representatives in connection with the report above given, a due regard for my official oath will not permit me to remain a silent spectator of the attempt thus made, to deprive electors of many counties in the State of their constitutional right to the voice and vote in your deliberations of their chosen Representatives, and the placing in their stead of persons who did not and cannot receive a majority of the votes in those counties.

It must be apparent to the mind of every person not blinded by prejudice, after fairly viewing our situation in the late past, and our present condition under civil government, that such action is a violation of the Constitution, which you and I have sworn to support.

When the armies of the confederated rebellion surrendered to the military power of the Government of the nation, and the persons composing the civil establishment of the insurrectionary States became either prisoners or fugitives, we were left a community composed of non-combatants, paroled prisoners of war, and persons—formerly slaves —who had been set free. *We were totally without political rights and privileges.* Those which we have since acquired are such as have from time to time been granted us by Congress.

Under the provisions of the Congressional law, *all male inhabitants* of the State, except such as were specially excluded by law, are permitted, after framing a Constitution acceptable to the General Government, to establish a government for the State.

All the rights, privileges and immunities enjoyed to-day by any citizen of this State, are so enjoyed under and by virtue of this Constitution, and are derived through the clemency of Congress in permitting us to organize a civil government under that instrument.

The attempt is now made to exclude electors who are not of Anglo-Saxon blood from the right of representing the voters by whom they were legally and constitutionally elected.

Whence does the elected Representative of one county derive authority to become a judge and decide that the Representative duly elected from another county shall not be seated?

If such authority is not found in this Constitution, it can only be derived from the unlawful exercise of power.

The only limitation upon the eligibility of an elector to office, or to membership of the General Assembly, is found in the following provisions of the Constitution of this State, and of the United States, namely:

CONSTITUTION OF GEORGIA.

Article I.

"SEC. 2 No person convicted of felony or larceny before any Court of this State, or of, or in the United States, shall be eligible to any office or appointment of honor or trust within this State, unless he shall have been pardoned."

"SEC. 4. No person who is the holder of any public moneys shall be eligible to any office in this State, until the same is accounted for and paid into the Treasury."

"SEC. 5. No person who, after the adoption of this Constitution, being a resident of this State, shall engage in a duel in this State, or elsewhere, or shall send or accept a challenge, or be aider or abettor to such duel, shall vote or *hold office* in this State; and every such person shall, also, be subject to such punishment as the law may prescribe."

"SEC. 6. The General Assembly may provide, from time to time, for the registration of all electors, but the following classes of persons shall not be permitted to register, vote or *hold office:*

First. Those who shall have been convicted of treason, embezzlement of public funds, malfeasance in office, crime punishable by law with imprisonment in the Penitentiary, or bribery.

Second. Idiots or insane persons."

Article I.

"SEC. 1, PAR. 4. No person holding a Military Commission, or other appointment or office, having any emolument or compensation annexed thereto, under this State or the United States, or either of them, except Justices of the Peace and officers of the militia, nor any defaulter for public money, or for any legal taxes required of him, *shall have a seat in either House ;* nor shall any Senator or Representative, after his qualification as such, be elected by the General Assembly or appointed by the Governor, either with or without the advice and consent of the Senate, to *any office*, or appointment, having any emolument thereto, during the time for which he shall have been elected.

"Par. 5. The seat of a member of either House shall be vacated on his removal from the district from which he was elected."

"Sec. 3, Par. 3. *The Representatives shall be citizens of the United States* who have attained the age of twenty-one years, and who, *after the first election* under this Constitution, shall have been citizens of this State for one year, and for six months residents of the counties from which elected."

Article IV.

Sec. 1, Par. 3. No person shall be eligible to the office of Governor who shall not have been a citizen of the United States fifteen years, and who shall not have attained the age of thirty years."

"Sec. 2, Par. 5. A person once rejected by the Senate shall not be re-appointed by the Governor to the same office during the same session or the recess thereafter."

Article V.

"Sec. 10, Par. 3. No person shall be Judge of the Supreme or Superior Courts, or Attorney General, unless at the time of his appointment he shall have attained the age of thirty years, and shall have been a citizen of this State three years, and have practiced law for seven years."

CONSTITUTION OF THE UNITED STATES.

Article XIV.

"Sec. 3. No person shall be a Senator or Representative in Congress, or Elector of President and Vice President, or hold any office, civil or military, under the United States, or under any State, who, having previously taken an oath as a member of Congress, or as any officer of the United States, or as a member of any State Legislature, or as an Executive or Judicial officer of any State, to support the

Constitution of the United States, shall have engaged in insurrection or rebellion against the same, or given aid or
comfort to the enemies thereof. But Congress may, by a
vote of two-thirds of each House, remove such disability."

CONSTITUTION OF GEORGIA.

Article XI.

"Sec. 1. *As the Supreme law:* The Constitution of the
United States, *the laws of the United States in pursuance
thereof,* and all treaties made under the authority of the
United States."

"Sec. 2. As next in authority thereto, *this Constitution.*"

From the foregoing it must be freely admitted that no
person is made ineligible under our Constitution on account
of race or color.

That *negros are citizens and electors* of the State, and,
therefore, entitled to all the privileges enjoyed by other citizens and electors, and subject only to the same restrictions,
is further demonstrated by Article I, Section 2, and Article
II, Section 2 of the Constitution, as follows:

Article I.

"Sec. 2. All persons born, or naturalized, in the United
States, and resident in this State, are hereby declared citizens of this State, and no laws shall be made or enforced
which shall abridge the privileges or immunities of citizens
of the United States, or of this State, or deny to any person
within its jurisdiction the equal protection of its laws. And
it shall be the duty of the General Assembly, by appropriate legislation, to protect every person in the due enjoyment
of the rights, privileges and immunities guaranteed in this
section."

Article II.

"Sec. 2. *Every male person born in the United States,* and
every male person who has been naturalized, or has legally
declared his intention to become a citizen of the United States,
twenty-one years old, or upward, who shall have resided in this
State six months next preceding the election, and shall have
resided thirty days in the county in which he offers to vote,
and shall have paid all taxes which may have been required
of him, and which he may have had an opportunity of paying, agreeable to law, for the year next preceding the election, except as hereinafter provided, *shall be deemed an
elector,* and every male citizen in the United States, of the

age aforesaid, except as hereinafter provided, who may be a resident of the State at the time of the adoption of this Constitution, shall be deemed an elector, and shall have all the rights of an elector, as aforesaid : *Provided*, That no soldier, sailor or marine in the military or naval service of the United' States, shall acquire the rights of an elector, by reason of being stationed on duty in this State; and no person shall vote who, if challenged, shall refuse to take the following oath : ' I do swear that I have not given, or received, nor do I expect to give, or receive, any money, treat or other thing of value, by which my vote, or any vote is affected, or expected to be affected at this election, nor have I given or promised any reward, or made any threat, by which to prevent any person from voting at this election."

I am aware that gentlemen argue that the eligibility of the colored elector to office should have been affirmatively stated by specific enactment in the Constitution, in order to vest in him that privilege.

It might, with more propriety, be argued, that a Constitution framed by delegates who were voted for by eighty-five thousand black men and twenty-five thousand white men, and ratified by the votes of seventy thousand black men and thirty-five thousand white men, did not carry with it that privilege to the white elector, because it was not *affirmatively stated*.

Admitting, however, that this privilege ought to have been so granted, we find that, by Paragraph 3 of Article XI of the Constitution, the Code of laws, known as Irwin's Code, continues of force, when not inconsistent with the Constitution.

Section 1648 of the Code is as follows : "Among the rights of citizens are the enjoyment of personal security, of personal liberty, private property, and the disposition thereof, the elective franchise, *the right to hold office*, to appeal to the Courts, to testify as a witness, to perform any civil function, and to keep and bear arms."

Section 1849 of the Code states that "all citizens are entitled to exercise all their rights as such, unless specially prohibited by law."

Sections 1850 and 1851 specially prohibit females and infants—both of which classes are citizens—from exercising certain of the rights of citizens.

Will any one declare that these sections are inconsistent with the Constitution?

Will any one deny that a negro is a citizen?

In the Constitutional Convention which framed the Constitution under which we act, on the 15th day of February, 1868, Mr. Waddell of Polk, moved a reconsideration of so much of the journal as related to the striking out of the 10th Section of the report of the Committee on Franchise, for the purpose of offering the following as a substitute for said section, namely: "*White men only* shall be eligible to office of trust, honor or profit, or employment, whether municipal, judicial or political, in this State, and *white men only* shall serve as jurors in the Courts." This motion was voted down by a vote of 103 to 19. If the Convention intended that *white men only* should hold office, why did they not adopt Mr. Waddell's motion?

Again, is it reasonable to suppose that a class of citizens, who had been recognized and commissioned as officers to execute the Reconstruction acts, by holding the elections, and who had been qualified as members and officers of the Convention which framed our Constitution, should be now any the less eligible under the Constitution which they participated in framing, unless the right they then enjoyed had been curtailed, or entirely withdrawn by express enactment?

No, gentlemen, the framers of the Constitution made no distinction between electors, or citizens, on account of race or color, and neither can you without violating it.

It is argued that this can be done under Paragraph 1, Section 4, Article III: "Each House shall be the judge of the election returns and qualifications of its members, and shall have power to punish them for disorderly behavior or misconduct by censure, fine, imprisonment or expulsion; but no member shall be expelled except by a vote of two-thirds of the House from which he is expelled."

Each House is the judge *only as to whether its members are qualified according to the provisions of the Constitution* and the laws made in pursuance thereof; but the House certainly shall not "judge" members to be ineligible or disqualified, because their political sentiments or the color of their skin is not acceptable to the majority; nor shall they, in case there should be a doubt as to the legitimacy of such an act, place the weight of that doubt *against the person on trial.*

Having first silenced, *en masse*, the votes of twenty-five of your members, and then by resolution, in defiance of the Constitution, declared them ineligible, you now propose to fill their places by citizens who failed to receive a majority of the votes in their respective counties.

Is that a Republican form of Government, where a minority of electors rule? Are not the privileges of a citizen "abridged" by your action? Does not the Constitution of the United States guarantee to each State a Republican form of Government, and to the citizens all their privileges and immunities?

Is it not the duty of Congress, by appropriate legislation, to enforce that Constitution?

Have we, from our past experience, any reason to believe that Congress will fail in its duty?

But, reasoning from motives of policy alone, the denial of the right of colored men to office will but stimulate a desire on their part, which has not heretofore existed, to press themselves forward into official positions.

As the result of an election for delegates to the Constitutional Convention, when none participated except the negroes and the few white friends of self-government who were not overawed by the opponents of Reconstruction, we find an assemblage of one hundred and sixty-nine members, of whom *only thirty-three* were persons of color; and in the late election, when every possible means were used to prevent white persons from becoming candidates on the popular side of the question, out of ONE THOUSAND TWO HUNDRED AND EIGHTY-THREE persons elected to office, only FORTY-FIVE of that number are colored.

Add to these facts that, with a General Assembly of two hundred and seventeen members, but thirty-one are colored, and it must be apparent to the unprejudiced mind that the colored men have not acquired that insatiable thirst for office which is so characteristic of our own race. The denial, however, of a well-established right will beget contention for the enjoyment of it.

In conclusion, I most respectfully and earnestly call upon you, as lovers of our common country and well-wishers of the peace and good order of the State, to pause in the suicidal course upon which you have entered, urged on as you are by bold, bad men outside your body, whose wicked counsels have once drenched our land in blood, and whose ambition now is to ruin that which they cannot rule.

RUFUS B. BULLOCK, Governor.

[The following extract from the published proceedings of the House of Representatives, is appended:]

"During the reading of the above Message, Mr. Burtz said it was disrespectful to the House. We had declared negroes ineligible, and let us stick to it. Let us vindicate our dignity and return the same to his Excellency.

"When the reading of the Message was concluded Mr. Duncan offered the following:

"*Resolved,* That the portion of the communication of his Excellency reflecting upon the action of this House in deciding upon the eligibility of free persons of color, under the Constitution, be returned to his Excellency, with the following resolution:

"*Resolved,* That said communication is not warranted by the resolution upon which his Excellency was requested to act, and that the Constitution declares that the members of each House are the judges of the qualifications of its own members, and not the Governor; they are the keepers of their own consciences, and not his Excellency.

"On the adoption of the resolution, the ayes were 71, nays 32.

"Mr. Bryant offered a protest against the seating of the white members *vice* negroes unseated. Not in order.

"Mr. Tumlin moved to swear in the members declared . elected *vice* the negroes declared ineligible.

"Mr. Rawls moved to amend by saying: Provided they are not men of color. Agreed to.

"Mr. Shumate moved to amend further: Provided they are not ineligible under the 3d Section, 14th Article Constitutional Amendment. Agreed to, and the resolution, as amended, was adopted.

"Mr. Shumate moved that Messrs. Harper of Terrell, Lee and O'Neal, be appointed a committee to examine into the eligibility of the new members under the Constitutional Amendment. *Not agreed to.*

"The following members appeared, were sworn and took their seats." [Here follow the names of the new members who were at once admitted and sworn, without reference to their eligibility or ineligibility under Article XIV of the Constitution of the United States.]

———

The following extracts are taken from the proceedings of the Constitutional Convention of Georgia, held in the city of Atlanta in the months of December, 1867, and January, February and March, 1868.

"FEBRUARY 24, 1868.

＊   ＊   ＊   ＊

"On motion of Mr. Blodgett the Rule was suspended for the introduction, by Mr. Whiteley, of the following resolution, which was taken up, to-wit:

"*Resolved*, That the Judiciary Committee be, and they are hereby instructed to report to the Convention, at an early day, an Ordinance declaratory of the qualifications of members of the General Assembly, at the first session thereof under the Constitution being adopted by this body, and that the qualification aforesaid shall be as follows:

"The Senators and Representatives shall be citizens of the United States who have attained, in the case of the former, to twenty-five years of age, and in the latter, to twenty-one years of age, and who have been inhabitants of the State of Georgia for a period of six months, and residents of the district or county from which elected three months immediately preceding the election.

"Mr. Bell of Banks, moved to amend by striking out the word 'inhabitants' and inserting 'citizens.'

"Mr. Blodgett moved to amend by inserting before the word 'citizens' the word 'male.' The motion was withdrawn by the mover.

"Mr. Trammell moved to amend by striking out all after the first clause.

"This motion was lost.

"On the question of adopting the amendment of Mr. Bell of Banks, the yeas and nays were required to be recorded.

"There were yeas 44, nays 63. So the motion to strike out the word 'inhabitants' and insert 'citizens' was lost.

"The resolution was adopted without amendment."

"FEBRUARY 25, 1868.

*   *   *   *   *   *   *   *   *   *

Mr. Akerman, from the Judiciary Committee, made the following report, to-wit:

"Under instructions from the Convention, the Committee on the Judiciary report the following Ordinance:

"An Ordinance declaratory of the qualification of members of the General Assembly, to be chosen at the first election held under the Constitution framed by this Convention.

"*Be it ordained by the people of Georgia in Convention assembled*, That the persons eligible as members of the General Assembly, at the first election held under the Constitution framed by this Convention, shall be citizens of the United States who shall have been inhabitants of this State for six months, and of the district or county for which they shall be elected for three months next preceding such election, and who, in the case of Senators, shall have attained the age of twenty-five years, at the time of such election.

"The foregoing Ordinance is not reported as the recommendation of the Committee, but simply in execution of the instructions of the Convention in the resolution passed yesterday. For the Committee.

"A. T. AKERMAN, Chairman."

MARCH 3, 1868.

*   *   *   *   *   *   *   *   *   *

"On motion of Mr. Akerman, the report of the Judiciary Committee on the subject of the qualifications of members of the first General Assembly, under this Constitution, was taken up.

"The previous question was called for and sustained.

"The main question was put, and the Ordinance reported by said Committee adopted without amendment.

"The same has been spread in full on the Journals of the Convention of a previous day."

[From the above extracts it will be seen that an Ordinance was passed by the Constitutional Convention specially stating that persons who are citizens of the United States, and *inhabitants* of this State for six months, are eligible to seats in the General Assembly.]

MESSAGE TO THE SENATE.

[Extract from the published Proceedings of the Senate]

THURSDAY, September 17, 1868.

The following Message was received from his Excellency the Governor, through Mr. Eugene Davis, his Secretary :

EXECUTIVE DEPARTMENT,
ATLANTA, GA., September 15, 1868.

To the Senate :

Your Secretary has presented to me the following :

"WHEREAS, The Senate having declared that T. G. Campbell who has held a seat as Senator from the Second Senatorial District, is ineligible to his seat; and that George Wallace, who has held a seat as Senator from the Twentieth Senatorial District, is ineligible to his seat as such; therefore

" *Resolved*, That the two persons in said Senatorial Districts, respectively, who received the next highest number of votes to the persons declared ineligible by the Senate, if eligible, are entitled to their seats as Senators from the Second and Twentieth Senatorial Districts.

2. " *Resolved*, That his Excellency the Governor be respectfully requested to transmit to the Senate a statement of the election returns for Senators in the Second and Twentieth Senatorial Districts of this State.".

Being, by the above resolution, requested to participate in an act which I conscientiously believe to be unconstitutional, it is due to my convictions of responsibility, under my oath of office, either to decline complying with that request, or, upon a compliance, to make known that I do so only in deference to the voice of the Senate, and to respectfully present the reasons which lead me to a conclusion opposite to that entertained by your body.

Some of these reasons were presented in a communication to the House of Representatives a few days since, and to this I desire to add but a few words.

It has been argued that the members of the Convention who framed the Constitution intended that colored men should be excluded from the privilege of holding office, and that the majority of the members understood that the Constitution did not *expressly confer* that privilege, and that, therefore, it did not exist.

Having been myself a member of that Convention, familiar with its organization and action, I feel at liberty to say that the argument above alluded to is not well founded, and that it is not sustained by the records of the Convention.

The great question that presented itself to the members of the Constitutional Convention, when assembled, was, "How can we best establish a Government for the State, under the spirit and letter of the laws by which we are assembled, that shall insure its being and remaining in full accord with the Constitution and Government of the United States, and at the same time secure for our State internal tranquility and prosperity?"

This could only be done by disqualifying and disfranchising, for official positions and from the franchise, the large class of persons who had exhibited opposition to the Government, first by armed rebellion, and later by refusing propositions which had been made, looking to restoration, by declining for themselves, and by urging others to abstain from participation in the election of Delegates; and restricting privileges of office and of the franchise exclusively to those who had evinced a desire for restoration to harmonious relations to the General Government; or, by adopting the more liberal and Republican policy of giving the ballot freely to all men, and with but few limitations, leaving the electors to be the judge of the *qualifications* of the person whom they might see fit to select by their votes to represent them.

Assuming that if all the male inhabitants of the State had a free voice and place in the new State Government, the majority would keep it in harmony with the National administration; that where all enjoyed equal civil and political rights, none could have just cause for dissatisfaction, the latter course was very properly adopted.

That this was done in good faith and with a full understanding by a majority of the members of the Convention, that colored men were no less eligible than white men, is clearly demonstrated by the journal of their proceedings.

Confining the argument simply to the eligibility to membership of the General Assembly, we find that by Section 3, Paragraph 3, of Article 1.

"*Representatives* shall be *citizens of the United States,* * * * * who, after the *first election under this Constitution,* shall have been *citizens of this State for one year.*" *
* * *

10

This section declared who should be eligible after the first election, and that there should be no doubt left as to who were eligible at the first election, the Convention, on the 24th of February, instructed the Judiciary Committee to report "an Ordinance declaratory of the qualification of members of the General Assembly *at the first session* thereof, * * * and that Senators and Representatives shall be citizens of the United States, * * * who have been *inhabitants* of the State of Georgia for a period of six months." * * * *

The word "inhabitant" was purposely used, believing that sticklers for "State Rights" doctrine would hold that the colored man did not become a *citizen* of Georgia until made so by our Constitution, and that, therefore, if required to be a *citizen* six months *previous* to the election, *that* requirement would exclude the negro.

The statement that this belief was well founded is sustained by the fact that a motion was made to strike out of the Ordinance the word "inhabitant" and insert "citizen."

On this motion the yeas and nays were called, resulting in 44 yeas and 63 nays.

It was, therefore, clearly the opinion of the *forty-four* that the use of the word "inhabitant" made colored men eligible to membership, and in this they were correct.

This Ordinance above referred to was reported by the Judiciary Committee, and adopted by the Convention without division, on the 25th of February.

While arguing the question, we should consider only *the law and the facts*, leaving out of view our preferences and personal judgment of the propriety or impropriety of colored men holding seats in the General Assembly.

For the reasons heretofore presented to the House of Representatives, and those herewith presented, I most respectfully object to the action heretofore taken, and that about to be taken by the Senate on this subject, as being at variance with, and violative of, the Constitution which we have sworn to support, and of the right of Senators who have been duly elected.

I herewith transmit the names of W. R. Gignilliat, of the 2d Senatorial District, and of Thomas J. Adams, of the 20th Senatorial District, as the persons who received the number of votes in their respective Districts, next highest to the number which elected T. G. Campbell, in the 2d, and Geo. Wallace in the 20th Senatorial Districts, as follows:

T. G. Campbell, Sen., received 1,256 votes, and W. R. Gignilliat, received 539 votes in the Second District; and

George Wallace received 2,654 votes, Thomas J. Adams received 1,263 votes, and Z. B. Roughton received 1,072 votes in the 20th District.

Rufus B. Bullock, Governor.

Mr. Candler offered a resolution that inasmuch as the Senate was the sole judge of the qualifications of its own members, and that a simple request had been made to the Governor, as the custodian of the election returns, to furnish the names of those elected in the place of those claiming the highest number of votes; therefore, that the portion of the message only giving the desired information be entered upon the journal, and the balance expunged.

Mr. Candler claimed that the Governor had, under cover of the Executive Department, insulted the dignity of this body. He publishes to the world that this body, no matter by what vote, has violated the Constitution, and also our oaths.

Mr. Brock rose and replied that he would vote against the resolution, as it was unjust to the Governor.

Mr. Merrell also spoke against the resolution.

Mr. Wooten advocated its adoption. His appeal to the twenty-four members who voted for the exclusion of colored men was a strong one, and by the forcible manner in which Mr. W. promulgated his reasons furnished evidence sufficient that he was in dead earnest.

Mr. Adkins followed in opposition, assuming the ground that we had no right to split the message, and if we did, the crime was committed, and the best way to get out of it was to make redress.

On the passage of the resolution, the yeas and nays were called for.

Those voting in the affirmative are:

Messrs. Anderson, Burns, Candler, Collier, Fain, Griffin of the 21st, Hinton, Holcombe, Lester, McArthur, McCutchen, Moore, Nisbet, Wellborn, Winn, Wooten.

Those voting in the negative are:

Messrs. Adkins, Bowers, Brock, Colman, Corbitt, Dickey, Griffin of the 6th, Harris, Higbee, Jones, Merrell, McWhorter, Richardson, Sherman, Smith of the 36th, Speer, Stringer, Welch.

So the motion was lost, and the Message of the Governor will be recorded on the journal.

The Senator from the Second Senatorial District, Mr. Gignilliat, appeared, was qualified and took his seat.

MESSAGE

OF

GOVERNOR R. B. BULLOCK.

EXECUTIVE DEPARTMENT, }
ATLANTA, GEORGIA, February 15, 1869. }

To the House of Representatives:

The following joint resolution, adopted by your honorable body on the 4th day, and concurred in by the Senate on the 8th day of February, instant, has been presented to me for approval:

"A RESOLUTION.

"WHEREAS, It is believed that a judicial decision of the question of the colored man's right to hold office in Georgia, under the Constitution now of force, would restore the State to her proper position in the Union, and give quiet throughout the State; and whereas, said question is one which the Courts of the State can properly take cognizance of; and whereas, we, the Representatives of the people of Georgia, are unwilling that any effort should be spared on our part to bring about a state of peace and happiness to the people, and a settlement of that important question; be it therefore

"*Resolved, by the Senate and House of Representatives of the State of Georgia, in General Assembly convened,* That a case involving the right of colored men to hold office shall, as soon as the same can be properly brought before the Supreme Court of the State, be heard and determined by said Court, and we believe that the people of the State will, as they have heretofore always done, in good faith, abide the decision of the highest judicial tribunal of the State whenever so declared."

It is with great regret that I find the resolution to be of such a character as to force upon me the unpleasant duty of returning it to your honorable body without my assent.

The desire which, it is believed, actuates both the Legislative and Executive branches of our State Government is so to shape our course that we may insure harmony between the two, and at the same time command the approval of Congress, and thereby obtain a recognition of our State Government as an integral portion of the American Union.

The Joint Resolution referred to does not, in my judgment, recommend itself as tending to bring about that very desirable result.

The Resolution does not settle, nor does it even touch upon, either of the two leading points at issue, viz: The organization of the Legislature under the law, and its subsequent action in excluding a large portion of its members on account of color.

The most prominent objection urged against the legislative branch is, that the original organization of the body was not made in accordance with the letter or the spirit of the laws of Congress which provided for its existence; and, next, that as a sequence to the non-execution of laws which were specially enacted to prevent such a result, the Legislature has assumed to expel a large number of its members, all of whom were known to be earnest and faithful adherents to, and supporters of, the Congressional policy, because of their "color," or "race," and seating in their stead, without an election by the people, of an equal number of citizens, all of whom were known to be opponents of that policy.

There cannot be a doubt resting upon the mind of any intelligent citizen as to the correctness of the presentment here made, of the obstacles which stand in the way of harmony among ourselves, and of our recognition by Congress as a State entitled to representation in the Union.

The evil results which have visited our people, growing out of our anomalous condition; the absence of proper restraints to insure the due protection of life and property, and the free and unrestricted expression of political opinion, are but the natural effects to be expected from the absence of properly organized civil government, and do not, therefore, enter into the question at issue.

First, then, let us consider whether the law covering the organization of the Legislature has been complied with. For the sake of reducing, as much as possible, the number of objections urged to the manner of organization, we will not discuss the requirements of any act of Congress prior to that of June 25th, 1868.

By that law, it is specifically enacted that "no person prohibited from holding office under the United States, or under any State, by section three of the proposed amendment to the Constitution of the United States, known as Article XIV, *shall be deemed eligible to any office in either of said States."*

It will not be admitted that a resolution adopted by a majority of your honorable body, to the effect that *all* sitting members were eligible under that law, was of sufficient force to decide in the affirmative a question which, it is alleged, would be, and is, negatived by the *facts* in the case of many of your members.

Can it be demonstrated that there are not now, and that there have not been since the organization of the General Assembly, many members participating in legislation *who took an official oath to support the Constitution of the United States, and afterwards gave aid or comfort to the enemies thereof?* If this cannot be done successfully, the legislative branch is clearly liable to the charge *of not having, in good faith, executed the law.*

So far as any action has been taken by Congress touching the status of Georgia, this position has been adhered to, and the result is that the action by the legislative branch upon the Constitutional Amendment and portions of the State Constitution necessary to our admission, is not yet recognized by Congress as valid.

The second point of objection made is upon the expulsion of members on account of "race," or "color;" members, too, who favored the system of government that was established under the authority of Congress; and the seating in their places of citizens who were opposed to that system, and who had been defeated at the polls by large majorities, thus, to that extent, practically subverting the government and silencing the voice of the people.

The views of the Executive as to the constitutionality or propriety of that course were, at the time of its adoption, communicated to your honorable body, and will not now be repeated.

As before stated, these are the more prominent obstacles which block the way to harmony and peace. The question which, as patriots and lovers of our country and our State, and advocates of their prosperity, we should unitedly and earnestly consider is, how shall these obstacles be overcome or removed?

The resolution under consideration ignores the question of original organization, and proposes action simply in the direction of asking a judicial decision upon the eligibility of colored citizens to office, without either pledging the body

adopting the resolution to abide by such decision in regard
to their own membership, or even *indicating a disposition*
so to do. In fact, it may be urged with force that a judicial
decision cannot be made effective upon the question of eligibility to membership in the General Assembly.

The laws at present in force are ample, and under them
any citizen, since the adoption of our present Constitution,
could have had the question tested before the Courts. Such
a case is now pending before the Superior Court of Chatham
County, and "the same will be properly brought before the
Supreme Court of the State, and *be heard and determined
by said Court*" without the intervention of a joint resolution
of the General Assembly, which, were it *mandatory*, might
be construed as being an improper interference by the legislative with the judicial branch of the Government.

The query naturally presents itself, why adopt a resolution which *practically* means nothing, and cannot effect any
thing?

I am unwilling to believe that your honorable body, in
adopting this resolution, intended to submit it to Congress
as the deliberate and *final* action of the General Assembly
toward the establishment of harmony among ourselves, and
with the National Government!

Are well-worded "resolves," which do not touch upon one
of the vital points at issue, and which have no binding force
as to the other, likely to satisfy a body of men, whose firm-
ness, wisdom and patriotism conducted the country successfully through the great rebellion?

May we not expect that Congress will ask stronger guarantees for the "rights, privileges and immunities" of over
five hundred thousand American citizens of the black race
who are among us, than the fallible judgment of three citizens of the white race?

After a careful examination of the whole subject, with the
aid of the light which has been shed upon it by the action
of Congress and of your honorable body since the opening
of your session, I feel constrained to renew the recommendation then made:—

"It is, therefore, respectfully recommended that we, our
selves, take the initiative in the consummation of the policy
of Congress, and acting upon our own sense of the obligation we owe to the authority from which we derive all we
now have or may expect to enjoy, of civil self-government,
undo what has been done."

"Restore the colored members to their seats, and exclude

every person from participation in your Legislature who took an official oath to support the Government of the United States, and afterwards gave aid or comfort to its enemies, until such person shall have been relieved by Congress of the disability thus incurred—bearing in mind that the only relief from such disability is found in the action of two thirds of each House of Congress, and cannot be accomplished by the individual opinion of the person affected, that the aid or comfort was not *voluntarily* afforded."

The adoption and execution of this course by ourselves. will, I am quite confident, secure for us full and complete recognition as a State in the Union.

RUFUS B. BULLOCK, Governor.

LETTER OF HON. W. B. FLEMING.

SAVANNAH, June 23d, 1869.

A. R. Wright. Esq:

MY DEAR SIR—Yours of the 21st instant, requesting me to give for publication in the *Chronicle and Sentinel*, my opinion upon the effect of the decision lately made by the Supreme Court of Georgia, upon the status of the expelled negro members of the present Legislature, is received.

I have no idea that my opinion will have, or indeed ought to have, any weight in "moulding public opinion," but as you desire it, and only because you desire it, I will give it. I can see no reason why this decision should have an effect different from other decisions. The decision of a Court, decides the case in which the decision is made, and of course becomes a precedent for the decision of other cases in which the same question arises. But who ever heard that the decision of any one case, decided every case involving the same question. There must be a separate decision in every case as it comes up. The case decided by the Supreme Court settles the question that White, although a negro, may hold the office of Clerk. It can have no other effect beyond the retaining of White in office, except as *authority* to control the decision of other cases as they arise involving the same question. But the decision will have to be made in every case. It cannot possibly have the effect to put in or out of office others who are strangers to the judgment. Is it not a well settled principle that a judgment binds only the parties to it? There are some cases in this county (Chatham), where white persons have been installed into office by the Ordinary, who, I think, very properly felt his duty to do so, under the decision of Judge Schley. Can it be that the effect of the decision in the case of White is to put them out and put the negroes in? Could a judgment of ouster be entered up against them on the judgment of the Supreme Court in favor of White? Can these negroes be put into office except by proceedings regularly instituted for the purpose? I think not.

The same, I suppose, is true of the negroes who were elected to the Legislature. The decision in the case of White cannot put them in, or the white men out, and for the simple reason they were not parties to that act.

And now comes the question, can the negroes elected to the Legislature make a case before the judicial tribunals of the State? I have no difficulty in saying *they cannot*. There is but one tribunal with jurisdiction to decide this question, and from the decision of that tribunal there is no appeal; it is final and conclusive, there being no other tribunal before which the decision can be reviewed or reversed. That tribunal is the Legislature itself. "Each House shall be the judge of the election returns and qualifications of its members, &c." Constitution Article 3, Section 4.

Respectfully, &c.,

W. B. FLEMING.

LETTER OF HON. M. J. CRAWFORD.

COLUMBUS, GA., June 24th, 1869.

General A. R. Wright:

DEAR SIR—Yours of the 21st instant, in which you ask my opinion upon the effect of the decision of the Supreme Court touching the eligibility of negroes to office, has been received. In reply, I have to say, that to the extent of their jurisdiction over the question, their decision will be binding and obligatory upon the people of the State. The trial and correction of errors from the Superior Courts of the State is the limit by the Constitution to that jurisdiction.

The effect, then, will be, in all cases where that tribunal has the *legal authority* to enforce their decision, to require that it be observed, and that negroes be installed into such offices as they may be elected to fill. But so far as the status of the negroes elected to the Legislature is concerned, that is not in the slightest degree altered or changed, because—by the Constitution—the qualification of members is *exclusively* given to the two Houses respectively, and from their *judgment* there is no appeal. No power is lodged anywhere by the organic law to review errors if they be committed in this respect by either of the Houses composing the General Assembly.

Their action in the premises, therefore, is final unless they should consent to reopen the question of the eligibility of the negro to their respective Houses, and upon argument had reversed their own decisions and adjudge him competent and qualified. To the extent that the members have respect for the judgment pronounced by the concurring Judges, they would give it consideration, and if sufficient to change their views, they would no doubt act in conformity therewith. But the whole matter rests necessarily in *foro conscienciæ*, and must be decided according to the individual opinion of members themselves. No man can, therefore, speak for another in such a matter, and whilst a majority of the present Legislature may be of opinion that the negro is ineligible, the very next may think and decide otherwise. The whole power over this subject is vested by the Constitution *permanently* in each House. It was not a provision made for a day or a case, but for all time, and therefore written in the organic law.

It has been thus in all Constitutions of all the States as well as in the Constitution of the United States from the beginning, and must of necessity be there so long as the present form of government stands.

But whilst I suppose this will be admitted, still the important question remains, what is the proper course to be pursued by the Legislature and the people? In my judgment, it is to render obedience to the law and the officers thereof, giving to the Legislature, the Executive and Judicial, each in its own sphere, all the rights, powers and privileges thereunto belonging, and in no case contravening them. By so doing the harmony of our governmental system will be preserved and the will of the people, where they are permitted, carried out. This necessarily throws upon the members of the Legislature the duty of disposing of this question of negro eligibility, and were I a member of either branch thereof, with my views upon the subject, I should vote unhesitatingly against it, and let consequences take care of themselves. This I should do conscientiously and in conformity to my opinion of the law, at all times, and in every form in which the subject might be presented.

But another and very important form in which this question may arise, is, in cases made before the Judges who are under the supervisory power of the Supreme Court, and whose decisions must conform under the law to those made by the higher tribunal. Over this class of officers the decision operates, and will be executed as the law until the same shall be changed by a reversal in the Supreme Court itself, or by the people in the manner prescribed by law.

I look upon the opinion of Judge Brown, even admitting his premises, as the clearest case of *non sequitur* that ever was written; in fact, illustrations, if such were ever collected, none could be found so apt as that pronounced by the Chief Justice in this case.

As to Judge McCay's, before he can make up his judgment he has to put us outside of all constitutions and laws, and take his start from that point. And with his theory he makes the negro a consistent element in the formation of the present State government, and, therefore, he has all the rights and privileges appertaining to any citizen of the Commonwealth. I confess that the negro constituted about ninety per cent. of the elements which made up the present Constitution of this State, the Federal soldiers with the bayonet about seven, and the remaining three per cent. was composed of native and imported whites.

The white element was, however, increased in the ratification of the Constitution, but this was due in a great degree to the clear and convincing argument of Judge Brown against the constitutional right of the negro to hold office.

But, taking Judge McCay's view, that we were outside, leaves me great difficulties to overcome. I cannot see how one from his standpoint can come to the conclusion that the Constitution of the United States had even become void or inoperative in these States, when the whole war was waged by the Federal Government upon the ground *that it was impossible for us to get from under its authority, and that it extended throughout the States and Territories of the whole*

Union. We were conquered into obedience thereto, and then for the first time it was discovered that it was not of force in these States; in its name we were denied its rights and privileges, and in its name the sword and not the judge declares the law. The inconsistency of coercing a State into subjection to the Constitution is only equalled by the enormity of the proposition that when she is coerced that the Constitution does not extend over it at all.

But to conclude our hastily written letter, we say that our duty is to obey the law as it is made and decided by each department of the government, *according to its power and authority to decide*, and make no effort to "disrupt the ties" &c., because the President prefers a "colored" to a "plain" Republican. With me a spade's a spade, and the "plain" will be for disrupting the—party unless the thing is stopped.

Respectfully yours, &c.,

MARTIN J. CRAWFORD.

————

LETTER OF HON. JUNIUS HILLYER.

ATHENS, June 24th, 1869.

General A. R. Wright:

MY DEAR SIR—I received by yesterday's mail your letter referring to "the recent decision of the Supreme Court of this State, in relation to the eligibility of negroes to hold office, and asking my opinion upon the effect of this decision upon the status of the expelled negro members of the present Legislature.

At your request, General, I willingly give you my opinion upon the question stated. In doing so, I think it best not to crowd the columns of your paper by an elaborate argument, but to content myself with a simple statement of my opinion, with such reasons and remarks as may be necessary to make it clear and intelligible.

I have all my life been a law-abiding man, and have made the principle of obedience to the laws of my country a part of my religion and a matter of conscience; and while I regard the Supreme Court of the State as the proper final ar-

biter of all questions which come within its exclusive jurisdiction, yet I am clear and decided in the opinion that the
decision referred to in your letter does not affect the power
and duty of each House of the General Assembly to deter
mine the right of the negro to seats in their respective
bodies.

There is no Court in this world which is clothed with
power or jurisdiction to judge of the election returns and
qualifications of the members of the General Assembly of
the State of Georgia.

The Constitution expressly devolves that high duty upon
each House to determine for itself. And when the Constitution declares that "each House *shall* judge of the election
returns and qualifications of its members," it means that
each House shall pass *its own* judgment according to the
view taken by it of the law of the case before it. It does
not mean that each House shall endeavor to make its views
conform to the *supposed* opinions of other departments of
the Government, but, like every other judicial tribunal, each
House is bound by the Constitution to announce its own
judgment according to its opinion of the law. And this
judgment, when announced, is final. From it there is no
appeal. The power is not given to reverse their own decisions, and in the case before us, in my judgment, the negroes expelled by the two Houses of the General Assembly
cannot be re-seated according to law. With them the case
is *res adjudicata*, and no tribunal has jurisdiction further to
act upon it.

It may be said that the Legislature ought to follow the
decision of the Supreme Court, as a high authoritative precedent. I don't think so. The question of precedent don't
apply in this case. It is expressly excluded. For the Constitution declares that the jurisdiction of the two Houses
shall be exclusive over the election returns and qualifications
of the members of each.

Each for itself—independent of each other, and independent of every other tribunal. It would be equivalent to
abrogating that salutary clause of the Constitution to adopt
the rule that the two Houses of the General Assembly ought
to follow the rulings of the Supreme Court in cases supposed
to be analagous. It would reduce that clear, comprehensive
clause to this absurdity, that "the two Houses shall judge
of the election returns and qualifications of their members
except where they have reason to suppose that the Supreme
Court would differ from them, and in all such cases they
shall decide according to what they think would probably

be the opinion of the Supreme Court." For it will be remembered that the Supreme Court have not decided that negroes are eligible to seats in the Legislature, and never can so decide, for the question never can be brought before it.

It has simply decided that a negro was eligible to be Clerk of the Superior Court of Chatham county, and it is *inferred* that two members of the Court are of opinion that negroes are eligible to the Legislature. And this is the authority which we are called upon to respect, when it is urged that every cautious judicial tribunal will always respect the adjudications of the same questions by other tribunals. When we come to view this decision in the light as authority and to consider how much weight should be given to it then we meet the important fact that it was made by a divided court—that the two Houses of the General Assembly may well inquire, and they ought to inquire (if they refer to the decision at all as authority), whether Judge Warner, the dissenting Judge, is not entitled to more weight, and his opinion, as a mere matter of legal authority, entitled to more respect by all careful, conscientious tribunals than both the other members of the Court together. In making this point I mean no disrespect to Judges Brown and McCay. It is a fact well known that in Georgia, on a point of law, Judge Warner's opinion would weigh down half the Bench and Bar of the State.

If precedent is to govern this question we may well inquire why the Supreme Court ventured to disregard the High authority of the two Houses of the General Assembly who were clothed in the Constitution with the jurisdiction to try and determine the question before them? Why did not the Supreme Court *infer* that the Senate and House were of opinion that under the laws of Georgia a negro could not hold office, and give effect to what they supposed to be an authority in point?

Here we have two decisions made upon what most persons consider analagous cases by two distinct tribunals, independent of each other, and both having jurisdiction to try the question made in the case before each. And strange to say the tribunal which rendered the first decision is called upon to reverse its own deliberate judgment and adopt the decision of the other tribunal. Can they do this without a virtual admission of their own intellectual inferiority?

I am aware that I have gone somewhat beyond the precise point made in your letter, which is confined to the status of the expelled negro members of the present Legislature. I am of opinion that as to them the decision of the two Houses is final and irrevocable, and they cannot be reseated without a violation of the law. I am further of opinion that in all future cases the Constitution makes it the duty of each House of the General Assembly to judge for itself of the election returns and qualifications ot its members. They are bound to pass *their own* judgment. They are not permitted to adopt the judgment of other departments of the government.

General, there are questions of policy and political results involved in the contemplated action of the Senate and House of Representatives that I do not wish to discuss. I greatly regret that there is reason to fear that our cruel conquerors, after compelling the members of the Legislature to swear that they will judge of the election returns and qualifications of their members, will then punish the people of Georgia because they will not violate their oaths by making a decision contrary to their judgment. Let the Legislature do what they believe to be right and let us all cheerfully abide the consequences.

JUNIUS HILLYER.

LETTER OF HON. A. M. SPEER.

GRIFFIN, GA., June 24, 1869.

General A. R. Wright:

DEAR SIR—Yours of the 21st instant, inviting an opinion from me "upon the effect of the decision of the Supreme Court upon the status of the expelled negro members of the present Legislature," has been received.

Permit me to preface my reply with the remark that considerations alone, personal to you, has induced me to make one. I have no desire to express, through the press, any political opinion; neither do I suppose that I could influence to any extent the action of the Legislature upon the question you propound by anything I might write.

Still, courtesy to you and a common desire with you to

see this question settled upon the basis of justice and law, forbids me remaining silent under the call you have made upon me.

Whether the recent decision made upon this subject accords with our own views, should not, in my judgment, influence the course we ought to desire adopted by the Legislature.

I am candid to say that my own opinion has been that the Constitution adopted recently for the State; conferred the right to hold office upon the negro. Such were the views entertained by most of the Democratic press—by the leaders and organs of the party, and it was made in the canvass one of the most prominent objections to the adoption of that Constitution by the people. Were we sincere then, or were we making an objection to a Constitution we did not think well founded? I cannot believe those who entertained those views *then* were acting insincerely with the people in urging an objection they did not believe existed. If they were our opinions then—and we so expressed them—I cannot see with what consistency or propriety we can now complain, that the decision sustains our opinions heretofore expressed. A majority of the Legislature, however, upon the question being made and discussed, entertained different views, and by resolution declared the colored members ineligible— their seats were vacated and the white members admitted.

As might have been anticipated, this course aroused the indignation of a large portion of the Radical party, and it has been made the excuse of groundwork for a determined and persistent effort to place the State again under military rule—have her civil government declared provisional and subject to the future action of Congress.

It has been the means of excluding us from a voice in the United States Senate, and has left some of our members of the Lower House dancing attendance as lobby members vainly seeking admission to seats for which they had been elected.

To break the force of this storm the action of the Legislature had raised against our State, they, by joint resolution, agreed to submit the question of the eligibility of the negro to the Supreme Court and *abide its decision.* This resolution passed both branches, and notwithstanding it met Executive opposition, and is not now a " legislative act," yet morally speaking, the Legislature are bound to abide by their own pledge.

Honesty and self-respect, in my judgment, leaves them no other alternative.

It is claimed that the decision of the Legislature as to these members is "*res adjudicata.*"

I do not understand that the rule of "*res adjudicata*" applies to legislative action.

The rule applies with all its vigor and force to the Courts of the country—for the policy of the law has been from time immemorial to settle and quiet controversies between its citizens—by the application of this rule.

But not so with the Legislature. The same session can review, modify, change or abrogate entire its former action. How often have we known again and again resolutions agreed to, modified subsequently, and finally rescinded.

There is a provision in the Constitution which forbids the same Legislature (at the same session) "from proposing (unless with consent of two-thirds) any bill, ordinance or resolution, intended to have the effect of law, which shall have been *rejected* by either House." But this does not extend to bills, ordinances or resolutions which have been *passed* or *agreed* to by either House."

The whole question, then, is subject to the action of the Legislature, and the rule of "*res adjudicata*" does not apply."

And such has been the uniform action of legislative bodies.

It has arisen in every case where a member has been seated, and afterward, upon investigation, declared ineligible. In such cases the Journals show the member has been found qualified and sworn. Subsequent investigation shows him ineligible, and he is removed. And yet, I have never heard the first action claimed as *res adjudicata*, and plead as bar to investigation and removal.

These negro members of the first organization were allowed to be sworn in. The Journals show (I presume) they were declared qualified and sworn as members. It was not claimed that the question was *res adjudica* when they were put upon trial, why, then, claim it in behalf of those who took their places?

One other view and I am done. The Legislature are the law-making power, but they *are not superior to law.* As a body, they are bound by the Constitution and laws, as every other body or citizen, until modified or repealed. The Constitution established a tribunal for the construction of laws, where a controversy arises, "The Supreme Court. To its mandate we all bow and give obedience. Shall it be said that this body may obey or not as they choose? I hope not. It is not a proper example to establish for our people. If they have erred on a question of law, and it has been so pronounced, let them show their perfect obedience to law by retracing their steps and conforming to the law as expounded.

It is true, obedience to law in their case may bring evil upon us in one sense—it may foist into office some utterly unfit, and displace (as in this case) others who are of priceless value to our councils. Let us accord in a spirit of justice and of obedience to law, every right the Constitution confers upon the colored race; it will be a moral triumph over our feelings and prejudices that will elevate the character of the Georgia Legislature for political and personal integrity, that in due time will bear the fruit of peace and stability, and go far toward crushing out the slanders upon us as a people.

Let not the Legislature rest upon a quibble that belongs to the Courts to justify a departure from the broad path of justice and right. If reckless legislation and unwise results follow this decision and its legal consequences, the great majority of the white citizens of Georgia are not responsible, and in due time, intelligence and worth and propriety will claim and take control. And we may then point with pride to this period in our history —when, amid the clamors of the thoughtless—the prejudices of race, and the evil results that threatened our State, the Legislature dared to do right.

I am, very truly, your friend,

ALEX. M. SPEER.

LETTER OF HON. J. W. H. UNDERWOOD.

ROME, GA., June 28, 1869.

General A. R. Wright:

DEAR SIR—Yours of the 21st instant, asking my "opinion upon the effect of the decision of the Supreme Court, relative to the eligibility of colored citizens to office upon the status of the expelled negro members of the present Legislature, has been received, and for answer I have the honor to say that the decision refered to of the Supreme Court cannot possibly affect the status of those members in any degree whatever. By the first paragraph of the 4th Section of the 3d Article of the Constitution of Georgia, it is provided that "Each House shall be the judge of the election, returns, and qualifications of its members, &c."

By the 31st paragraph of the 2d Article of the same Constitution it is declared that, "The Legislative, Executive and Judicial Departments shall be distinct; and each department shall be confided to a separate body of magistracy. No person, or collection of persons, being of one Department, shall exercise any power properly attached to either of the others, &c.

It seems, therefore, to be exceedingly clear that the Senate and House of Representatives, each House separately for itself, has the sole right and power to judge of the qualifications of its members, and the power to interfere is expressly denied to the judiciary department.

The question of the eligibility of the colored members of the General Assembly has been fully considered and decided by the two Houses, the proper tribunal having original, exclusive and final jurisdiction over the question; the decision has been rendered and the judgment executed. There can be no appeal or writ of error to any other Court, and no provision is made for a new trial, and the question is closed forever.

No precedent is remembered by me of a rehearing in such a case—either in the State Legislature, the Congress of the United States or the British Parliament. Nor is it believed that there is one. There is nothing peculiar in this case to render it an exception to an unvarying rule of law, and the usage and practice of centuries.

The decision of the Legislature was made in a case where the jurisdiction is undeniable, and with which all interference is expressly forbidden, and other persons whose eligibility is unquestioned, hold the seats—and hold them legally, by the judgment of the only department having a right to judge, and cannot be disturbed in the exercise of their rights. The balance of the term of the present Legislature is short, and no reason is perceived for any change.

With very high respect,
Your obedient servant,
J. W. H. UNDERWOOD.

LETTER OF JUDGE E. G. CABINESS.

FORSYTH, June 24, 1869.

General A. R. Wright:

My DEAR SIR—You request me "to give you, for publication in the *Chronicle and Sentinel*, my *opinion* upon the effect of the decision of the Supreme Court of this State in relation to the eligibility of negroes to hold office upon the status of the expelled negro members of the present Legislature."

By the Constitution "each House is made the judge of the election returns and qualifications of its members," and from the decision made by either House there is no appeal. No tribunal has been created with power to supervise the judgment of the two Houses in regard to election returns and qualifications of their respective members, and when a decision is made ousting a member from his seat in either House, the decision is conclusive so far as that the member ousted can take no appeal from it and no other tribunal has jurisdiction of the case.

The effect, then, of the decision of the Supreme Court holding negroes to be eligible to hold office does not necessarily restore to their seats the negroes who were removed for want, in the opinion of both Houses, of eligibility to office.

The decision of the Supreme Court cannot act upon the judgment of the Legislature and reverse it. That judgment must stand unless it should be reversed by the bodies which rendered it. And that is now the practical question which the Legislature must meet when it reassembles. Shall the negroes who were removed from their seats be restored, and can the two Houses of the Legislature reverse their action.

In my opinion, they can, and policy requires that it should be done.

No judgment has been passed by either House upon the *right* of the *successors* of the removed negroes to the seats they occupy. Upon the removal of the negroes, those who claimed their seats were held *prima facie* entitled to them, and were seated accordingly. No question as to *their* right to their seats was raised, and never has been decided.

If their right to the seats they hold should be contested upon the ground that other persons eligible to office, received a higher number of votes than they did respectively, would it not be competent for each House to declare them not entitled to the seats they occupy, and would it not follow, as a matter of course, that the persons eligible to office, (and it must now be considered a settled question that negroes are), would it not necessarily follow that such persons having received the highest number of votes should be admitted to their seats? Recollect that no decision has been made, and no judgment rendered, fixing the successors of the negroes in their seats. There is no *res adjudicata* as to their rights to seats. Let the question be raised whether *they* are legally entitled to membership, and in the present aspect of matters and the present state of the law, and what we must receive and recognize as law, it would be competent for each House to declare them not entitled to seats, and readmit those who received the highest number of votes. And policy requires that this should be done. We must submit to whatever it is not in our power to correct. If we had control of this question of negro suffrage and negro eligibility to office, we would give it a different direction, and would soon lay it at rest. But it is not under our control. A power which we cannot resist is giving and will give it direction, whether rightfully or not, it matters not now to say. It is sufficient for us to know that this power is in active exercise, and will be until this question is finally settled, as "the powers that be" desire it.

Let us raise no more questions with it. All the issues which we may make with the United States, upon the terms of Reconstruction will be decided according to their will, and not ours. And they have the power to enforce their decisions. Let us submit to inevitable necessity, however bitter the pill, and make no more issues with power.

It is related of the Emperor Adrian, who reigned in the decline of the Roman Empire, that one day he found fault on a point of grammar with a learned man of the name of Favorinus. Favorinus could have defended himself and justified his language, but continued silent. His friends said to him, "why didn't you answer the Emperor's objections?" "Do you think," said the grammarian, 'that I am going to enter into dispute with a man who commands thirty legions?"

Is it wise to continue to raise questions with a power which can command as many legions as may be necessary to enforce its will?

Not only the peace but the good of the whole country requires that all questions connected with Reconstruction should be settled as speedily as possible. It is Reconstruction and the issues growing out of it, which preserve the unity of the Republican party. In Reconstruction they "live and move and have a being." Strip them of the support which this question gives them, and their dissolution will speedily follow. You "take their life when you take the means whereby they live."

Though negro suffrage and negro eligibility to office may be distasteful to us, let us submit to them without further opposition, if by so doing we can put a stop to these questions, and thus destroy the bond of unity which holds the Republican party together.

Very respectfully.

E. G. CABINESS.

————

LETTER OF HON. WARREN AKIN.

CARTERSVILLE, June 29, 1869.

General A. R. Wright:

DEAR SIR—Yours of the 21st instant, asking my opinion as to the effect of the decision of the Supreme Court of this State in relation to the eligibility of negroes to hold office, upon the status of the expelled negro members of the present Legislature, is received and considered.

I do not see how it is possible for the decision of the Supreme Court rightfully to have any effect on the action of the Senate or House of Representatives any more than the decision of each House could rightfully effect the decisions of the Court. The State Constitution declares that "each House shall be the judge of the election returns and qualifications of its members." Each House, in passing upon the qualifications of a member, decides for itself; and neither the Executive nor Judiciary department of the Government can review, or call in question the correctness of the decision when made. When the Senate or House has decided that a member is not entitled to the seat he occupies, and that another person is, the decision is final and conclusive. The House itself, after deciding that a member is not constitutionally qualified to hold a seat in the House, and turns out the sitting member, and decides that another is qualified and entitled to the seat, cannot legally reverse its decision, and put back the expelled member. Each House is "the *judge* of the qualifications" of its members, and when *judgment* has been pronounced, and the time for reconsideration is passed, the right to the seat is *settled*, and cannot again be reviewed or reversed. The Supreme Court sometimes makes mistakes, and when discovered, reverses former decisions, but the rights of the parties as settled by the erroneous decision, remain unchanged. Suppose at the December term of the Supreme Court another case should come before it, involving the same question recently decided, and after full argument and mature consideration, the Court should reverse its decision, and hold that a negro is not eligible to office in Georgia, would this decision have the effect to turn out of office the negro in Chatham county, who now holds office under the decision and judgment of the Court? Every lawyer knows it would not. If it would not have that effect when the Supreme Court makes both decisions, much less could it do so when the former decision was made by a distinct tribunal, the judgment of which cannot be reviewed by the Court.

The decision of the Supreme Court should have great weight with either branch of the General Assembly; and if after the next meeting of the Legislature, each House should pass a resolution acknowledging its error, and the members now occupying the seats formerly held by the negroes should resign, (and I have heard it said that they ought to do so,) this would not reseat the expelled negro members. The resignations would create vacancies, which alone could be filled by election. Neither House can elect or appoint a member to fill a vacancy. The people must do that, and expelled members have sometimes been re-elected by the people.

I do not wish you to understand that, in anything I have said, the correctness or incorrectness of the decision of the Supreme Court is called in question. My opinion as to the right of the negro to hold office under the State Constitution is generally known in this section of Georgia. I did not hesitate to express it, more than a year ago, and I have not changed it.

I have written hurriedly, and have not time to elaborate the views expressed. They are at your service, while I remain very truly yours.   WARREN AKIN.

LETTER OF GEN. LAWTON, JUDGE HARDEN AND HON. THOMAS E. LLOYD.

SAVANNAH, July 1, 1869.

General A. R. Wright:

DEAR SIR—We severally and duly received your circular letter of the 21st ult., requesting of each of us an opinion upon the effect of the recent decision of the Supreme Court of this State "upon the *status* of the expelled negro members of the present Legislature." Presuming it will be equally agreeable to you to receive our united opinion, we present the following unanimous answer to your inquiry:

By the Constitution of Georgia it is declared that "each House shall be the judge of the election returns and qualifications of its members," &c. It is apparent, therefore, that the decision of either House on the question of eligibility of a member of that House is the judgment of the only tribunal to which the Constitution has entrusted the question. The *status* of the expelled negro, as to eligibility to the Legislature, cannot, therefore, be affected by any decision of the Supreme Court.

You will not understand us as at all denying the right of another body of Senators or Representatives to determine differently as to the qualifications of a negro to sit in the General Assembly. All we mean is to express our opinion "upon the *status* of the expelled negro members of the *present* Legislature."

We are, very truly, your obedient servants,

EDWARD J. HARDEN,
THOMAS E. LLOYD,
A. R. LAWTON.

LETTER OF HON. ALEXANDER H. STEPHENS.

LIBERTY HALL,
CRAWFORDVILLE, GA., June 29, 1869.

General A. R. Wright, Chronicle & Sentinel Office, Augusta, Ga:

DEAR SIR—Your letter of the 21st instant was duly received, but it found me in worse condition physically than I have been for several weeks. This, with other pressing correspondence, has prevented me from giving you my opinion upon the question propounded, sooner.

I must now be brief. Indeed there is no necessity for any extended views. The argument is already exhausted by you, your neighbor of the *Constitutionalist*, the *Constitution* at Atlanta, the letter of Judge Fleming, and the communication of Tully in your paper, some days ago, to say nothing of the labors and productions of others. But in what I have to say, it is proper to premise by stating that I believe the decision of the Supreme Court on the question of negro eligibility to office in this State to be in accordance with the law and Constitution which were their guide. Had I been on the Bench I should have come to the same conclusion under the same law and Constitution, that a majority of the Court did, though not exactly by the same process of reasoning pursued by these learned Judges. The result of my judgment, however, would have been the same.

I thought the two Houses of our General Assembly committed an error in deciding that those members who had been elected, and returned to their respective bodies with an eighth or more of African blood, were thereby disqualified to hold seats in the Legislature under the laws and Constitution of the State as they now stand. But it was a question which they alone—each House for itself—had the right and power under the Constitution to adjudicate and determine. By the Constitution of the State, each House is made the sole judge to decide upon election returns and qualifications of its members. This question of eligibility and qualification to hold office on the part of this class of persons, who are elevated to the *status* of citizenship by the present Constitution of the state, I knew was one not free from doubt, one on which able and true men might and did differ. Therefore, while I thought the decision to be erroneous, I also thought that all charges against these Legislative bodies upon the grounds that their judgment had been made from captious and factious motives were altogether unjust.

This now clearly appears from the able dissentient opinion of Judge Warner, an eminent jurist of the Republican Party, who still maintains, after all the discussion since had, that the decision of the Houses was right. Men on both sides, therefore, should learn to be more charitable in their opinions of the motives of men in the discharge of public duties.

But your question to me is, what effect this decision of the Supreme Court now rendered, can have upon the cases of those members, who were decided by the respective

Houses of the Legislature, not to be qualified to hold seats therein? Will it be to *reseat* these excluded members, or are they *legally entitled to be reseated thereby?* To this there can be but one legal and judicial answer. That is, no! These cases have been decided by the only tribunal having constitutional jurisdiction over them, and having been decided they cannot again be opened even by the Houses who decided them. Their judgment after being finally rendered cannot be again taken up or reversed by themselves, any more than the Supreme Court itself can go back to the docket of last session and reverse any of its own judgments then rendered to the unsettling of the rights of parties therein adjudicated. Much less can this judgment of the Supreme Court legally affect in any way the action of the two Houses in the premises. It can have no binding or obligatory effect whatever upon the past or future action of the houses of the General Assembly upon the question involved, for by the Constitution, as stated above, each House is the sole and exclusive judge of this question so far as membership of their respective bodies is concerned for all time to come, or so long as the Constitution shall remain as it is on that point. No change, it is presumed, will ever be made in it in this particular, for it is in strict conformity with that universal law in all representative governments whenever and wherever established, either civil or ecclesiastical, by which the *sole power* to decide *absolutely* upon the qualifications of the members of the Legislative bodies is and has been, without exception I believe, vested in those bodies themselves. From their decision there is no appeal to any other tribunal; and from the very nature of the subject there cannot properly be. This power, like all other delegated powers, has often been very grossly abused in this as well as in other countries. It has been grossly abused repeatedly, perhaps, by one House or the other of the Legislature, in every State of the Union, as it has unquestionably often been most grossly abused by Congress. Its gross abuses in the British Parliament are well known by students of history. Still this arrangement in the distribution of the powers of Government is the only one, or the best one, yet discovered for keeping separate, distinct and perfectly independent of each other the three great Departments, to-wit: the Executive, Judiciary and Legislative. Monstrous as the doctrine seems to some, yet it has come down to us stamped with the wisdom of our ancestors after the experience of centuries.

This sole power to decide upon the election returns and qualifications of the members of each House which is vested in it by the Constitution, is however, by no means an unlimited power. Because there is no appeal from its exercise, this by no means justifies a capricious or illegal decision under it. It is a power of great trust to be exercised as all other judicial powers are. Each House is constituted a judge for the purpose—this Court so constituted is to hear and decide both the law and the facts in each case as it comes before them. First, to hear the facts and then apply the law to them. In forming their judgment upon the law and the facts, they are to be governed by the same general principles which govern all other courts in arriving at truth, right and justice. Their decisions when made in any case stand as the decision of all other courts, from which no appeal or writ of error lies. This is the law of the case.

But how far members of the Legislature might very properly be influenced (in deciding doubtful questions of law involved in the legal qualifications of those elected and returned to the respective Houses) by the judgment of the highest judicial tribunal in the State upon the same questions in all other offices of the State, *is a very different question.* My opinion is that in all doubtful questions, or where their own convictions are not both clear and strong, they should be influenced, but not otherwise. The two Houses of our General Assembly at the last session, I have been informed, concurred in a resolution submitting this question as one on which they had doubts, to the Supreme Court, with a pledge to conform to the decision of that Court in their action. How this is, I do not know, but if my information is correct, it certainly relieves them of all imputation of improper or factious motives in their first action. The effect of the decision now rendered under that resolution, would be a requirement of them in all future like cases which may come before them to decide, in accordance with the principles established by the judgment of the Supreme Court. This is all the fulfillment of the pledge that they can legally and constitutionally render. This, I think, the same Judges who made the decision would, if inquired of, pronounce to be the right view of the subject.

Yours most respectfully,

ALEXANDER H. STEPHENS.

LETTER OF A CORRESPONDENT IN THE MACON TELEGRAPH.

THE DOCTRINE OF "RES ADJUDICATA" IN ITS APPLICATION TO LEGISLATIVE BODIES.

Editors Telegraph: Since the decision of the Supreme Court, in White's case, declaring negroes eligible to office there has been considerable discussion with regard to its effect upon the "legal status of the expelled negro members, and of the *power* and *duty* of the Legislature to reseat them."

Thus far the discussion has been confined principally to the question, "Has the Legislature the *power* to reseat the expelled negro members?"

The majority of the writers support the negative of the question upon the ground that the proceedings of the Legislature under that clause of the Constitution which makes it "the judge of the election returns and qualifications of its members" are judicial in their nature, and that a resolution declaring any member ineligible is "*res adjudicata*" and, therefore, a bar to all future action upon that case.

As no precedents have yet been cited on either side, the writer desires, through your columns, to call attention to a notable and essential parallel case, as well as to the rules of a law applicable to and supporting the affirmative of this question.

The *power* of the Legislature to "judge of the election returns and qualifications of its members" is one given it "to guard its own rights and privileges from infringement, to purify and vindicate its character, and to preserve the rights and sustain the free choice of its constituents," (1st Story on the Constitution, Paragraph 833,) and possessing the *power* it has the *right* to so regulate its rules of proceedings that the *objects* for which the power was given, may be attained. This right has been exercised by legislative bodies both in the United States and Great Britain, from time immemorial, and is one concerning which there can be no controversy, for no one believes that our people have been guilty of the great absurdity of *proposing an end and denying the means to attain it.*

Having this right, the only question which requires to be answered, in determining its *power* to reseat the expelled members, is, *has the Legislature adopted the rule of "res adjudicata," as a part of its code of procedure in contested election cases?* The journals do not show that this rule has ever been before, or acted upon by, the Legislature; it certainly was not pleaded in bar to the resolution passed last session, submitting the negro eligibility question to the arbitration of the Supreme Court, nor was it urged by the Georgia delegation, when before Congress, as a defence of the action of the Legislature in not reseating these members. And therefore, in the absence of any evidence tending to prove the adoption of this rule, it is fair to say that it never has received Legislative sanction. As it has not been *expressly adopted* by the Legislature, it cannot be applicable to and binding upon it, for the reason that it is a rule originating with and established by courts of law, for the purpose of protecting the rights of persons as settled by judicial decisions. Without this rule courts could never make an end of litigation between parties, give credit and stability to their decisions, or in any way accomplish the ends for which the judiciary is designed.

The Legislature, on the contrary, can best protect itself and the rights of its constituents, by inquiring into the "election returns and qualifications" of its members, whenever, and as often, as the circumstances of each case may require.

A case involving the same principle arose in Congress in 1837, known as the "Mississippi Contested Election Case." The facts are as follows: The President of the United States convened an extra session of Congress in September, 1837. This was the first session of the Twenty-Fifth Congress. As the regular congressional election in Mississippi did not occur till the November following, the Governor of the State issued a proclamation fixing a day for an election of members *for the extra session*. The election was held, and Messrs. Gholson and Claiborne were returned. When their names were called at the organization of the House, objections were made, but were overruled, and the subject was referred to the Committee of Elections, with the instructions contained in the following resolution:

" *Resolved*, That the Committee of Elections be instructed to report upon the certificates of election of Messrs. Claiborne and Gholson, the members elect from Mississippi, whether they are members of the Twenty-fifth Congress or not. And that said committee take into their consideration the proclamation of his Excellency Charles Lynch, Governor of said State, and the writ of election issued in accordance with said proclamation on the 13th day of June, 1837; and, also, the act of the Legislature of Mississippi entitled 'An act to regulate elections,' approved March 2, 1833."

The matter received thorough investigation, and upon the evidence adduced, Messrs. Gholson and Claiborne, by a written argument submitted to the committee and subsequently furnished to the members of the House, claimed their seats in the House during the Twenty-fifth Congress; and a majority of the committee thereupon made a report to the House which concluded with the following resolution:

" *Resolved*, That Samuel J. Gholson and John F. H. Claiborne are duly elected members of the Twenty-fifth Congress, and as such are entitled to their seats."

This resolution was reported on the 25th of September, and after a lengthy discussion was adopted on the 3d of October.

In November the regular Congressional election was held in Mississippi. Messrs. Prentice and Word were the only candidates, and received a majority of the votes cast for members of Congress, *but less than half of the votes polled at that election*. At the next session these gentlemen appeared as contestants for the seats of Messrs. Gholson and Claiborne. The whole matter was again referred to the Committee of Elections, and, after thorough investigation, *which elicited no new facts*, a majority of the Committee reported the following resolution, viz:

" *Resolved*, That the resolution of this House of the 3d of October last, declaring that Samuel J. Gholson and John F. H. Claiborne were duly elected members of the Twenty-fifth Congress, be rescinded, and that Messrs. Gholson and Claiborne are not duly elected members of the Twenty-fifth Congress.

This was reported on the 12th of January, and on the 16th "made the special order of the day for this day, and of each succeeding day, at one o'clock, until the same shall be decided."

Mr. Claiborne submitted a written argument setting forth their claims to their seats. He claimed that although the House had the right to unseat them, yet to make its action consistent it ought to abide by its former decision.

The question was discussed daily until the 31st of January, when the above resolution was adopted.

Among those who voted to seat and then to unseat these members, appears the name of that able constitutional lawyer, the Hon. James M. Mason, of Virginia.

By Article 1, Section 5, of the Federal Constitution, it is

provided that "each House may determine the rules of its proceedings;" and acting under this authority Congress has always adhered to the ancient rule and reconsidered its action in cases of contested elections, whenever the circumstances of any case seemed to demand it. Although this power which is given Congress in express terms, is, under our Constitution, an implied one; yet, it has always been exercised by our Legislature, and considered as essential to preserve its independence and freedom of action, as its power to judge of the election or qualifications of its members; for neither without the other would be of any practical utility.

The results, then, of our inquiries may be summed up as follows:

1. The Legislature has the power to "determine the rules of its proceedings."

2. In determining these, it has adhered to the ancient parliamentary rule of reconsidering its action whenever, and as often as the circumstances of each case may render it necessary.

3. Therefore, *the Legislature has, under the rules of its proceedings, the power to reseat the expelled negro members.*

Since so much has been said about the rule of "*res adjudicata*" a few words with regard to its applicability to the case in question, may not be out of place here.

"*Res adjudicata,*" (thing decided) a term adopted from the civil law— is defined to be a "legal or equitable issue which has been decided by a court of competent jurisdiction." The "*rule*" is that the issue then decided is binding upon the parties, and a bar to all further proceedings, on their part, concerning the subject matter thereof. But to make a matter "*res adjudicata*" there must be a concurrence of the four conditions following, namely:

1. "Identity in the thing sued for:" 3 East, 346.

2. "Identity of the cause of action:" 6 Wheat, 109.

3. "*Identity of persons and parties to the action:*" 7 Cranch, 271. 1 Wheat, 6. etc.

4. "Identity of the quality in the persons for or against whom the claim is made:" 4 Term, 490, etc.

The Legislature, in reconsidering its action in the case of the expelled members, will doubtless first inquire into the eligibility of those who now occupy their seats.

To this action, then, must we apply the test of "*res adjudicata.*" By the 3d condition, above stated, there must be an "*identity of persons and parties to the action.*" But these new members were not parties to the action of the

Legislature when the negroes were expelled; therefore, the rule of "*res adjudicata*" cannot be pleaded in bar to these proceedings.

This new investigation would show that the negroes, and not the new members, were legally elected.

The new members, to sustain their claims, would then plead the ineligibility of the negroes by reason of "color." This would bring in issue the whole question of negro eligibility, without any action on the part of the expelled members, so that even if the rule of "*res adjudicata*" was binding upon Legislative action, it would not be applicable to the case in question.

But, as we have seen, the Legislature has the power to reseat these members—a power founded on reason, dictated by the soundest policy, and by a long series of precedents.

How, then, unless this power be exercised, can it, under all the circumstances of the case, "purify and vindicate its own character, and preserve the rights and sustain the free choice of its constituents?"   B.

TABLE OF CONTENTS.

—— ••• ——

[NOTE.—Page 103 contains a brief statement of the case, as made by Judge McCay when delivering the judgment of the Supreme Court. For ready access to the *facts* it will be found particularly useful.

The Record of the Court below is printed in the order of arrangement in which it was presented to the Supreme Court. For greater convenience of reference, however, a somewhat different order is observed in the following analysis.—E. D.]

ARGUMENTS OF COUNSEL BEFORE SUPREME COURT:

OPINIONS OF THE JUDGES AND DECISION OF COURT:

APPENDIX.

CONTENTS

LETTERS.

LETTERS of distinguished legal gentlemen of Georgia as to the effect of the decision of the Supreme Court, upon the *status* of the expelled colored members.